Leadership:
The Art of
Motivation

The Sunday Times 'Business Skills' series currently comprises books on total quality management, personal skills and leadership skills.

This first class series has received a warm welcome from readers and critics alike: the opinion of Christopher Lorenz of the *Financial Times*, for example, is that it is 'excellent . . . well worth reading'. It is designed to build into an essential management library of authoritative and handsomely produced books. Each one, providing a definitive stand alone summary of best business theory and practice in its field, is also carefully co-ordinated to complement *The Sunday Times* 'Business Skills' video training package of the same name produced by Taylor Made Films.

BOOKS IN THE SERIES:

Leadership: The Art of Motivation

by

Nick Thornely and Dan Lees

C

CENTURY
BUSINESS

First published in the UK 1993
by Century Business
An imprint of Random House UK Ltd
20 Vauxhall Bridge Road, London SW1V 2SA

Random House Australia (Pty) Ltd
20 Alfred Street, Milsons Point
Sydney, NSW 2061, Australia

Random House New Zealand Ltd
18 Poland Road, Glenfield
Auckland 10, New Zealand

Random House South Africa (Pty) Ltd
PO Box 337, Bergvlei, South Africa

Set in Bembo by SX Composing Ltd, Rayleigh, Essex
Printed and bound in Great Britain by Mackays of Chatham, Chatham, Kent

A catalogue record for this book is available from the British Library.

ISBN 0-7126-5646-4

Acknowledgements

We would like to thank the following people who gave generously of their time and help during the preparation of this book:

Richard Phillips, Ashridge Management College; Michael Bichard, Benefits Agency; Anita Roddick, The Body Shop; Tony Lear, Brent Borough Council; Robert Evans, British Gas; Susan Hoyle, British Railways Board; Paul O'Hea, Terry Gough, Colt International; Ray Evans, Hall Harrison Cowley; Alastair Black, Karen Tully, Robin Walker, IML Employee Involvement; Mike Jones, Roy Prescott, Lakeside Training & Development; Diane Farrell, Rebecca Jenkins, Lane Group; Molly Lees; Steve Tanner, Prudential Assurance; Julian Richer, Richer Sounds; Ian Raisbeck, Bill Cockburn, David Rhodes, Royal Mail; the staff of Taylor Made Films; Jim Hale, Texaco; Alan Dawson, Toyota; John Neill, Unipart; Claude Lambshead, University of Bristol; Wendy White, Worthing District Health Authority; Dr Kurimoto, Yamazaki Machinery.

Contents

Introduction

It is easy to recognise a highly motivated organisation and to appreciate the apparently effortless way in which its members co-operate to achieve excellence in the service they provide for others and in the quality of life they themselves enjoy.

From the first contact it is evident that such organisations crackle with controlled excitement and that their managements have created a colourful, lively environmment in which people are moving towards challenging but attainable goals on the way towards an ever elusive perfection.

Invariably, all our dealings with organisations of this sort confirm our first impression that the warmth of their welcome is as genuine as their desire to please us by surpassing our expectations.

Such organisations, we discover, are 'companies' in the deeply significant sense of the Latin word 'com-panis' which the Romans used to describe an association of companions with whom they broke 'panis' or bread.

In companies like these, one feels, nothing is too much trouble and any worries are transformed into challenging problems which everyone helps to solve.

The highly motivated company is unmistakeable. It is invariably among the most profitable in its field and is imbued with a soundly based self-confidence that is never allowed to deteriorate into arrogance. It is an organisation whose name the whole workforce uses with pride and, most of all, an organisation in which people enjoy what they do and consider such a state of affairs to be entirely natural.

Many such companies exist and much of this book is devoted to a detailed examination of their practical approach to motivation.

To place their achievements in context we also look at motivation in general, examine the changes in motivation techniques over the years, consider the classic theories and put forward a few ideas of our own. Our hope is that this review of best practice in a wide variety of organisations will enable others to access their magic and to realise that in today's world any investment in motivation should be expected to yield not only profit but also a dividend of delight.

1. The Business of Motivation

The business of motivation is the motivation of business – and in this context motivation refers to the application of the forces which cause people to move, act, change and develop as individuals and groups. All organisations must be motivated if they are to survive and evolve and, basically, the problem of motivating the workforce of a company is the same as that of motivating a primitive tribe to gather food and to hunt. However, while today's managers can learn from the ways in which people were motivated in the past, it is our own culture which determines what motivates us, even though in essence the motivating forces remain unchanged.

THE MOTIVATING FORCES

The word motivation comes from the Latin word 'movare', meaning to move. Motivation produces movement and, as many managers will appreciate, it is movement which enables us to distinguish between the 'quick' and the 'dead'.

Our efforts to motivate ourselves and others are part of a natural, continuous and universal process which evolved into a balanced system for 'arousing, sustaining and regulating human and animal behaviour'. In fact many of the things which motivate us are the same as those which motivate animals. Like them, we can be motivated by purely physiological stimuli such as hunger, thirst and pain, but at the other end of the spectrum only Man can be motivated by things of the spirit and by the 'noble cause'.

ORGANISING THE WORK OF THE 'LEARNING ANIMAL'

Man is a learning animal and there is evidence that even at the hunter gatherer stage he had already begun to learn how to organise his work, although the dominant motivating factors were still those of pleasures like the excitement of the chase and the satisfaction of a full stomach.

THE FIRST MANAGERS

Among the things our ancestors were motivated to learn was the need for co-operation when hunting game. Hunting involved working in teams, which in turn motivated the choice or imposition of a leader, a person with the knowledge, experience and personality to coach and direct younger or less experienced hunters; in other words – a manager and a motivator. These were the earliest managers and it is unlikely that they needed to use pain or the threat of pain to motivate any but the dullest and most idle of their people. Instead they were able to promise them pleasures and satisfactions in the form of food, excitement, companionship, involvement, appreciation and many other benefits which would not be articulated for many centuries to come.

THE BEGINNING OF THE ORGANISATION

Sadly, when people abandoned the nomadic, hunter-gatherer way of life they gave up motivating mainly by pleasure and satisfaction and began motivating predominantly by pain and fear; the effects of this change – which also saw the beginning of 'them' and 'us' – were so traumatic as to give rise to the legend of a 'fall' or an eviction from Paradise in almost every culture. Ever since, the story of motivation has been that of a gradual return to the principle of motivating by pleasure.

Summary

- Early Man was motivated mainly by the 'carrot' of pleasure but the first 'managers' assumed that as the stick worked for animals it would also work for the managed.
- Today a different blend of carrot and stick (CAS) factors is needed if we are to utilise human resources to the full, and modern motivation is predominantly 'carrot' oriented.

Action!

- Identify the carrot and stick factors you are currently using to motivate your people. Are you using too many carrot factors or too many stick factors?

2. Motivation and the CAS Ratio

For managers the business of motivation consists largely of achieving the best possible ratio of 'carrot' to 'stick' motivation (CAS Ratio) for their organisation. However, though the basic carrot and stick concept of motivation is simple, 'the psychology of motivation', as Professor Frederick Herzberg put it, 'is tremendously complex'. The main reason for this complexity is the fact that 'everything motivates', but in practice, managers need only consider those factors which will lead to quantifiable improvements in productivity, savings, profits and company status.

MOTIVATING MOVEMENT

The potential complexity can be demonstrated by considering a few of the factors which influence an individual's actions in an everyday situation – like getting up to go to work.

Get Up	*Stay in Bed*
The sun is shining	It is raining
We feel great	We feel terrible
We have slept well	We have slept badly
We can smell coffee	We can't, or we can and hate it
An interesting morning ahead	The morning looks boring
Our partner is singing	Our partner is complaining
A good drive in prospect	Traffic problems to face
Miss Smith's smile	Mr. Jones' carping
We fear losing our job	We have sick time due

| The alarm is ringing | Damned alarm. I'm no slave |
| The house is snug | The house is cold |

The Butterfly's Wing Factor

Managers, whose main concern in the 'get up–stay in bed' situation is to ensure that their people get up in the morning feeling fit, happy and enthusiastic about the prospect of a day's work, may find the idea that 'everything motivates' disconcerting.

In practice, many motivating factors are 'butterfly's wing' factors. Their effect is usually so slight as to be negligible and it is re-assuring to note that motivation specialists now recognise the existence of only seventeen major categories of motivation factor.

Incidentally, as everything motivates, either positively or negatively from the point of view of the motivator, there is really no such thing as a demotivating factor but the word 'demotivate', meaning to demoralise, is so useful and so readily understood it would be a shame to lose it.

Motivating at a Distance

For managers the interesting thing about the factors which motivate people to go to work is how many they can control or influence.

Managers can influence, for example, the individual's financial position, with all that implies in terms of domestic comfort and harmony. They can also control many factors connected with the working environment, like physical surroundings and inter-personal relationships, and arrange to provide stimulating challenges and other job related satisfactions.

In other words, the motivation of a workforce begins long before the people concerned leave home.

Mapping Motivation

When considering the practical problems of motivation, there is a series of questions which can help simplify matters. These are the 'W' questions, the 'Who?' 'What?' 'Why?' 'When?' and 'Where?'

which make it possible to map out a motivating effort and create a managerial structure in which it will be most effective.

THE WHO? OF MOTIVATION

WHO do managers want to motivate? Human beings of course; but it is easy to forget that we are dealing with individuals so complex that out of the millions alive at this moment no two are exactly alike.

In addition, the WHO? of motivation is complicated by parental background, nationality, education, training and status – in other words the cultural background of the WHO? with all its attendant baggage of knowledge, prejudices, traditions and convictions, reinforced by a lifetime of group activities and pressures.

Countering the effects of people's culture – especially in the case of employees locked into traditional 'them' and 'us' attitudes – is difficult. Although motivation techniques help, the problem can be reduced from the beginning by effective personnel management. In fact, the WHO? is one element of the sequence which managers can control to a great extent and it is important that you should, if you are able, HIRE THE BEST, TRAIN THE REST AND – GET RID OF THE PEST.

THE WHAT? OF MOTIVATION

The second question is WHAT do you want to motivate people to do? Do you want to motivate an individual or a group to carry out a specific action or do you want to motivate your whole workforce to give of their best by improving their morale?

Deciding exactly WHAT? you want to do, or WHAT? you want other people to do, provides a goal, which is motivating in itself.

THE WHY? OF MOTIVATION

Deciding exactly WHY? you want to motivate other people to act in some particular way can be important.

Do you really want – or need – to motivate a particular action at all? Is it the correct thing to do? Is it in tune with your organisation's culture and your own view of what is right and wrong? Asking WHY? helps keep you in control.

The When? of Motivation

The WHEN? of motivation provides a timescale and a target. Do you wish to begin your motivating effort right now – or some time in the future – and do you intend to achieve some specific goal within a certain time? The WHEN? also governs the 'culture' of the WHO? as none of us is motivated in the same way as our grandparents. Similarly, our sons and daughters will often need to be motivated in ways different from those we found acceptable.

The Where? of Motivation

At its simplest, WHERE? is an environmental question.

Managers can motivate for instance by changing the decor of the work areas, moving machines or furniture, landscaping the approach to the workplace or improving rest room or catering facilities.

More important is the way motivation is affected by geography in such a way that the WHERE? affects the WHO? This is easy enough to appreciate if you are motivating, say, a workforce recruited in Papua New Guinea which would not be motivated in the same way as one recruited in Detroit; it could be more difficult to appreciate the cultural differences between, say, a workforce composed mainly of Londoners and another mainly of Yorkshiremen.

'Keep things Relatively Simple' – A. Einstein

Motivation is neither as simple as it appears at first sight nor quite so complicated as it begins to appear on more mature reflection. Albert Einstein advised that 'everything should be made as simple as possible – but not more simple' and to achieve this what we need are a few 'Laws of Motivation'.

SUMMARY

- The business of motivation is the motivation of business and the motivation of business is largely a question of determining the optimum CAS – or Carrot and Stick – Ratio and deciding how best to achieve it.
- Everything motivates either positively or negatively but common sense helps us to eliminate most minor factors.
- Managers can simplify matters still further by keeping their aim in view at all times and judging the likely motivating effect of various factors on such things as company profit, company wellbeing, company survival and company evolution.
- Motivation factors motivate either positively or negatively from the point of view of the person who is doing the motivating. This means that there is really no such thing as a 'demotivating' factor but the word 'demotivating' is so useful and so readily understood that it makes sense to retain it.
- The W Questions: Who? What? Why? When? and Where? determine the How? of motivation and help us map out our motivating strategy.

ACTION

- Make a list of the factors which affect or might affect a current problem of motivation in your own workplace. List 'motivators' and 'demotivators' and take note of any factors which might be both, depending on the 'Ws' involved or on the amount and quality of the respective factor.
- Decide on a goal towards which you wish to motivate yourself or others – either in the workplace or away from it. List some motivating factors you might use and set yourself a time limit.

3. The Laws of Motivation

The motivation of business is both an art and a science: a people skill and a body of knowledge derived from hands-on practical experience. Most managers have people skills of a high order and these can be improved by learning new techniques.

By contrast, the scientific approach to the motivation of business seems at first to be purely pragmatic, a series of motivating strategies based on the experience of successful motivators.

However, motivation is so closely allied to 'motion' that we can adapt the Laws of Motion propounded by the 18th century mathematician and astronomer Sir Isaac Newton. Substituting a human 'body' or 'bodies' – i.e. members of your workforce – for Newton's 'body' may give the text a certain tongue-in-cheek flavour but, in fact, business motivation is a question of getting people to move, a body is a body, and Newton's Three Laws apply to the human sort as well as any other.

NEWTON'S FIRST LAW OF 'MOTIVATION'

- Newton's First Law of Motion asserts that: UNLESS ACTED UPON BY A NET FORCE A BODY STAYS AT REST AND A MOVING BODY CONTINUES MOVING AT THE SAME SPEED IN THE SAME STRAIGHT LINE

It's not unusual for frustrated managers to think of some members of their workforce in precisely these terms and even respected academics have been known to wax nostalgic over the days when physical force was an acceptable motivator. However, the importance of Newton's First Law in the context of business motivation is that with its use of the word 'NET' it cuts through the complexities engendered by the fact that everything motivates either positively or negatively.

Net Motivation

If you are to motivate others, you must find a way of exerting a NET force in the direction in which you want people to move. It is the difference between the motivating forces you are able to exert and the force exerted by any negatively motivating factors which will determine the direction in which any particular 'body' will move and the speed with which he, she or they will do so.

Maximising Net Motivation

Maximising NET motivation is an important function of management and one which is made easier by the fact that managers are able to direct the thrust of their motivational effort as well as getting rid of undesirable negative factors. By contrast, it would be unusual – though not unheard of – for the people managers want to motivate to introduce negative or 'demotivating' factors deliberately. Instead, what many managers have to cope with is inertia defined as 'the tendency of a body to preserve its state of rest or uniform motion unless acted upon by an external force.'

Revealingly, 'inert' with its everyday meaning of 'inactive, lazy or sluggish' is derived from the Latin word *'iners'* meaning unskilled and today's practical motivators like the Bosch company, which employs 170,000 people in 130 countries, have banned the word 'un-skilled' as demotivating.

Newton's Second Law

- Newton's Second Law of Motion states that: A NET FORCE APPLIED TO A BODY GIVES IT A RATE OF CHANGE

OF MOMENTUM PROPORTIONAL TO THE FORCE AND IN THE DIRECTION OF THE FORCE

This suggests that it is easier to change the momentum and/or direction of a body – an individual or group – once it is moving, however slowly, in roughly the required direction.

This idea is borne out by practical experience. Most managers are already motivating their people to some extent – otherwise they would not remain managers for long. What is needed in most cases is a change of direction and an increase in momentum.

QUANTIFYING MOTIVATION

You can now give every factor you consider important an 'M' value, which will be either positive or negative (+M or −M) i.e. motivation in the desired direction or the opposite.

If you take '0' as being the M value of the infinitely small number of things which neither motivate nor demotivate then you can list each factor on a scale of say -10 to +10.

This will enable you to handle factors like 'salary' or 'recognition', both of which can be either positively motivating or negatively motivating according to how much or how little of either there is around.

Returning to the example of what motivates people to get out of bed and go to work, dealing with M factors in this way means that there is no longer any need to make separate lists of those factors which motivate people to stay in bed on the one hand and those which motivate them to get up on the other. Instead of considering 'The sun is shining' as a motivating 'Get up!' factor and 'It is cold and rainy' as a demotivating 'Stay-in-bed' factor, we can simply list 'Weather' as a motivator and assign to it an M Value which will be either positive or negative.

Once you have made your list of motivators and assigned M Values to each you need only add the figures together to find your NET motivation.

Newton's Third Law

- Newton's Third Law of Motion asserts that: TO EVERY ACTION THERE IS AN EQUAL AND OPPOSITE REACTION

This implies that if you want to motivate others you have to be careful not to provoke an adversarial situation in which, for example, the managerial pronouncement 'You will do this!' arouses the knee-jerk reaction 'Oh no, we won't!'

The Third Law implies that managers should avoid this type of confrontation wherever possible, which they can do by harnessing existing forces rather than by opposing them. In this way they can tap the reserves of talent and enthusiasm which are present in all organisations and at the same time make everyone's work more interesting and meaningful. This provides the basis for one of the prime rules in the motivation of business, namely that – IF YOU WANT TO MOTIVATE EFFECTIVELY YOU MUST 'INVOLVE TO SOLVE'.

Involve to Solve

The INVOLVE TO SOLVE rule encapsulates one of the recurring themes of modern motivation. It means that people at all levels should be empowered to make decisions and to be responsible for them. In a company which practises total involvement there are no more 'hands' and no more 'lower orders'; instead everyone is treated – and therefore tends to behave – as a responsible, intelligent and informed adult.

In our examples of best practice we shall be looking in detail at the mechanics of involvement and how the Involve to Solve rule is being implemented by successful and highly motivated companies. It is an essential element in the motivation of any company that seeks to survive hard times and to evolve when times are favourable.

Involving to solve does not mean 'soft' management, nor is it an invitation to the people on the shop floor to 'goof off'.

Involvement is an essential motivational tool – imposed by

enlightened self-interest – which enables top management to get on with the job of policy making, reduces the amount of middle management supervision required and provides stimulating challenges for the formerly satisfaction starved lower echelons.

THE NEW MOTIVATORS

Without exception, the highly motivated organisations we quote as examples of best practice rate involvement high on their list of motivating factors, but for centuries managers resisted any form of involvement on the part of their employees.

Even Robert Owen, who was so far ahead of his time that in the early 19th century his textile mills at New Lanark were a model of best motivating practice, drew the line at any form of worker involvement, while as late as the 1960s a leading American businessman wrote that there was no way he was going to 'allow the monkeys to run the zoo.'

Today, while there are still some managers who are less responsive to the motivating potential of involvement than others, most now see it as the way forward into the 21st century.

INVOLVING FOR THE THIRD MILLENNIUM

Backed and subsidised by the French National Electricity authority, the giant French aluminium makers Aluminium Dunkerque have built what they claim to be 'the industrial plant of the Third Millennium', a 5.7 billion franc smelter in which worker participation is such a strong element that the hierarchy has all but disappeared.

The automated plant employs few shop floor workers compared with plants built even a few years ago but, as a matter of policy, almost all the 600 workers were recruited from the ranks of the local unemployed and trained from scratch.

They are well, but not excessively, paid by French standards, with an average basic shop floor wage of 110,000 francs. All employees underwent extensive – and expensive – training before the plant became operational and most of them are capable of tackling any job which may arise.

THE POLICY

Aluminium Dunkerque's corporate policy includes:

- developing increased skills so that each employee can operate, maintain and manage complex equipment as well as being able to cope with future technological developments.
- the setting up of self-managed teams using clearly defined objectives but with autonomy which allows team members to make use of their individual skills.
- joint problem-solving methods to investigate malfunctions and improve quality and safety.
- salaries based on applied skills and the ability to develop a second trade.

An ergonomic approach to work stations and landscaped gardens come as part of the package, and the company claims that it is 'creating the perfect conditions for employees to use their professionalism, initiative and team spirit in a common endeavour to attain the plant's goals'.

TOO GOOD TO BE TRUE?

Worker enthusiasm is high and the unions have been cautiously welcoming, but there is some scepticism from outside the firm and one French professor of economics commented, 'All this harmony is too good to be true.'

In fact, all the organisations we cite as examples of best practice have already achieved bottom line success by involving to solve in ways which suit their own operation, and while some may not have gone quite as far as Dunkerque Aluminium others have taken involvement even further.

BACK TO THE PLEASURE PRINCIPLE

Involving to solve is one of the ultimate expressions of the Pleasure Principle which ensured that our hunter-gatherer ancestors did the work they needed to do, not just because it supplied them with food, but because they derived pleasure from it.

SUMMARY

- Newton's Three Laws of Motion, which concern the effects of varying forces on the movement of 'bodies', can be applied to motivation.
- NET Motivation is the sum of all relevant positively motivating and negatively motivating factors. The aim of management is to produce positive NET motivation i.e. motivation in the desired direction.
- Eliminating the 'equal and opposite' reactions of 'them' and 'us'. The Third Law as applied to industrial relations.
- The plant claimed to be 'a model for the 21st century' – an example of 'involving to solve'.

ACTION

- Keep a check on how many times you consult people further down your particular hierarchical pecking order, making a written record of Who?, Why? and the result. Make a conscious effort to involve people in this informal way.
- Identify some of the more important M Factors – i.e. positive motivating or negative motivating factors – in your own organisation and quantify them as either +M or −M Factors. Adding the figures will give you an indication of your NET Motivation and suggest the appropriate thrust of any additional motivating effort.

4. Motivating with Money – and Without it

Ask most people what motivates them and their first answer will be – 'Money'. Then they give the question some thought and in most cases decide that they are driven by many other motivating factors of equal or greater importance than financial reward.

When we were talking to Paul O'Hea, the energetic Managing Director of Colt International, about the high level of motivation he has generated in his company, we sprang the question on him: 'OK, that's what motivates the company – but what motivates you?'

He replied at once 'Money – I'm really motivated by money.'

Then he thought for a few moments and qualified his answer. 'Well, in fact I'm motivated 55 per cent by success and 45 per cent by the financial rewards.

'I may be one of the new breed of young manager. For my father I think it was 98 per cent satisfaction and the money was irrelevant. The overriding factor is the continuity of Colt as a privately owned family business. I could have had a much higher paid job in the City but knowing that families depend on my making the right decision is immensely satisfying.'

In much the same way, a man who had worked as a skilled craftsman in an aircraft factory looked at us as though we were mad to ask what motivated him and replied scathingly 'Money. All I'm interested in is what's in my pay packet at the end of the week.'

He then told us, almost in the same breath, how demotivated he and his workmates had been when it was decided to move their machines from a building with windows overlooking a stretch of parkland to an area with no natural light.

'It wasn't that we wanted to look out all the time, but it was good to be able to glance out occasionally. We were never told why we had to move. We suspected it was to make us keep our heads down but if that was the case it didn't work.'

Later he went to work for a small firm, and he told us about the day he asked the boss about the growing pile of scrap in the factory yard and suggested that he could find a good home for it. 'The boss told me to go ahead, so I rang up a couple of local schools and spoke to the metal-work teachers. They were round with vans almost before I put the phone down. I got a real kick out of making the suggestion and carrying it through myself,' he said, adding a few moments later, 'I don't make anything like the money I did before, but I enjoy going to work a lot more.'

NOT BY 'BREAD' ALONE

Like most people, both the wealthy Managing Director and the less wealthy shop-floor worker at first overestimated the value of money as a motivating factor in their working lives, but were prepared on reflection to revise their opinion.

However, the fact that people are motivated by other factors than financial rewards does not mean that money can be discounted or even treated lightly as a motivator. Money can generate very high M numbers, both positive and negative.

True, most of your people will not be motivated by 'bread' alone, but these days it's difficult to live without an adequate supply of it. As Buck Rogers points out in 'The IBM Way', the computer giant didn't build up one of the greatest sales organisations in the world solely by 'caring' for its people, because, while caring helps, it takes money to build homes, to educate children, to pay for cars, boats and holidays and to provide for a secure old age.

CARROT AND STICK

Money is an integral part of most workplace motivation packages. It can be used as payment in order to motivate, while the threat to deprive people of it can also be an extremely powerful motivator, especially in the short term.

AN AMERICAN NIGHTMARE

Some years ago, a privately owned American company was paying its creative people nearly twice as much as they could have earned elsewhere, and did its best to persuade them that their status demanded that they drive expensive cars and live in large and luxurious houses. Once the employees became used to a near millionaire life style, the boss showed the whip by threatening them with the sack, and by sacking one or two to keep the rest on their toes – so much so that Friday night was known to the staff as 'the night of the long envelopes'. Another of the boss's 'motivating' ploys was to berate senior employees, usually within the hearing of their colleagues, and then announce that he was cutting their salary by several thousand dollars. The original salary was almost always reinstated within a matter of weeks, by which time the employee was usually putting in a 14 or 15 hour day, seven days a week and hating every minute.

This style of motivation, which worked in the short term but provoked a huge and expensive turnover in staff, would have seemed perfectly logical to most of the entrepreneurs who created the industrial world we have inherited – and not all that foreign to their heirs of just a few decades ago.

MONEY AND THE MILLS

It was money that motivated people to work, and to send their children to work, in the 'dark satanic mills', and it was money that forced women and boys to work half naked as two-legged draft animals in Britain's coal mines. They had no choice.

What some younger managers find difficult to remember is that the Industrial Revolution is so close to their own time that only three life spans cover the whole industrial era, from the first machine-using cotton mills to the assembly lines and computers of today. For much of that time the motivation employed in most business enterprises was the same as that used by the early entrepreneurs – and that motivation was money and the fear of losing it.

MONEY MOTIVATES CHANGES

It was money which fuelled the 500 years of modernising changes between the Europe of illiterate serfs and peasants, ruled by kings and feudal lords, and the coming of the machines.

It was money that drove the mercantilism which provided Europe – and especially England – with the means to build factories and the know-how to market their products.

It was money which was to give England a huge advantage in the early days of industrialisation by encouraging the enclosure of open fields for profitable sheep farming. This turned the vast mass of English smallholders, who were tenants by custom only, into landless wage labourers who were then motivated to flock to the towns and to work 14 hours or more a day in the new factories.

THE MIXED BLESSINGS OF THE MONEY MOTIVE

The benefits of the Industrial Revolution were enormous. Driven by money, business provided the machines, the markets and the science which, in the industrialised nations, largely put an end to famine, plagues, illiteracy and much of the abject poverty still to be seen in parts of the Third World. However, the price included periodic unemployment, urban squalor and, on the factory floor, the growth of 'alienation' – a sense that it was all meaningless.

THE REAL REVOLUTION

Curiously, the Industrial Revolution, by forcing the agricultural workers away from the harsh physical labour of the fields towards the equally hard and if anything more repetitious work of the factories, would eventually bring about the revolution that would change the WHO? of motivation for ever.

In order to run the factories and mills efficiently, some of the workers, especially the foremen and supervisors, had to be taught how to read, write and do simple calculations – a need which led eventually to the institution of near universal elementary education.

Enlightened self-interest demands that business should offer the motivation of education and training to all those capable of benefiting from it and today's most highly motivated and successful companies are doing this.

Missionaries may have helped the people of what we now call The Third World to read in order to facilitate their work of conversation – enlightened self-interest again – but it was industry that motivated Third World youngsters to read, write and calculate, and it is modern business which is now sending them on management courses. It is in this way that the Industrial Revolution and the educational revolution it brought in its train have changed the WHO? today's managers need to motivate.

Summary

- Money is the most important single motivating factor in industry and business but there are many other factors which managers must consider.
- Early industrialists, themselves motivated by money, used it as a way of applying 'carrot and stick motivation'.
- Early industrialists tried to give their workers a restricted education to make them more useful, thus beginning a secondary revolution which is still affecting motivation methods.

Action

- Estimate in percentage terms the extent to which you are motivated by money. Then consider it (with your partner if you have one) and revise your estimate if necessary.
- Make similar estimates for your company and for your staff.

5. So You Think You Have a Motivation Problem?

For managers, the business of motivation is to motivate business – but what is it exactly that you want to achieve?

Of course you want to be able to use motivation, in the words of management guru Frederick Herzberg, 'to get employees to do as you want' – but what exactly is it that you want them to do?

Naturally the specifics will vary, but most managers would be content if they were able to motivate their people to give of their very best during the time they spend in the workplace.

YOU ARE ASKING A LOT . . . BUT

AS a manager you are asking your people to devote a third of their lives to your enterprise, often over the space of close on half a century – and what is more, to do so with enthusiasm.

Whatever the rewards and compensations on offer as the employer's part of the deal, they ought to be sensational.

In fact, you might be forgiven for thinking that finding motivation strong enough, not only to get people to do their jobs well but to be enthusiastic about them, is a daunting task. But it is a long way from being the toughest motivation job ever tackled: for as long a time as men have been motivating other people to work, they have also been motivating them to fight and die.

A MATTER OF LIFE AND DEATH

In the developed world at least, most managers no longer require their employees to risk their health, their safety, or their lives as an integral part of their job.

Of course there are people like policemen and firemen whose jobs entail an element of physical danger, but even they do not face the same risk of injury and death as those who take part in what was once the principle business of Mankind and is still, sadly, a substantial element of the world's activities – namely warfare.

At this moment people are being motivated sufficiently strongly to risk injury and death in half a dozen wars around the world. This has been the case for thousands of years, during which, for much of the time, war offered most of the available managerial challenges. Until long after the days of sail, for example, the Royal Navy was the biggest employer of labour in Europe.

The ways in which people are motivated to risk their lives are instructive for today's managers who merely wish to motivate in the workplace, especially as the factors which motivate men to fight have now changed dramatically because of changes in the WHO?

FIGHTING FOR £-S-D

Before the industrial era the motives which persuaded men to risk their lives in battle were reasonably straightforward.

They included at various times: xenophobia, fear of enemy attack, religious antagonism, the promise of manumission for slaves, devotion, often based on expectations of reward, and – rarely for the ordinary fighting men – loyalty to a city or nation state.

However what usually made men risk their lives were things like the prospect of glory or increased status, excitement, and most of all the certainty of some hard cash or its equivalent and the prospect of more as the prize of victory.

The Ultimate in Motivation

In 1914 when Britain went to war with Germany hundreds of thousands of young and middle aged men swamped the recruiting offices, desperate to enlist.

This in itself was an extraordinary feat of motivation but is perhaps easier to explain than the motives which inspired the same men, a month or two later, to leave the relative safety of their trenches in face of murderous machine gun and shell fire for the sake of a few yards of mud. The horrors of trench warfare, the indescribable conditions and the futile sacrifices made by millions of ordinary men are a matter of record and we are not suggesting that the battles of attrition were anything other than horrific waste.

However, the motives which persuaded men to join up in the first place and eventually to go 'over the top' were strong ones, so much so that managers will find many of them worth considering in the context of more peaceable objectives.

Motivation Without Money

The men who flocked to the colours in 1914 were not motivated by money. Apart from the unemployed, all the men who joined up – except for the fortunate ones whose wages were made up by their employers – were financially worse off than in their civilian jobs, and knew that their families would face considerable hardship.

Why did they go in the first place? Ironically it was the change in the WHO? brought about by near universal elementary education which made them an easy target for the motivators. They had been taught to read, taught to be patriots, and were readily influenced by the jingoistic popular press.

M Factors That Retain Their Power

A list of some of the factors which made people join up will enable you to decide which are relevant to your motivation effort.

1. The recruits were persuaded that they were part of a great enterprise and were engaged in a NOBLE CAUSE.

    This is still one of the most powerful of motivations. You should make it clear to your people that, by serving others, you and they are working together in a NOBLE CAUSE. Where possible involve the whole organisation, including yourself, in community projects. Presenting 'Quality' as a worthwhile cause enabled it to be seen as motivating – which it is – and explains the success of TQM.

2. The war itself was an EVENT on a huge scale, probably the most exciting thing which had happened in the recruits' lives.

    EVENTS, as an antidote to routine, are an important motivating tool. If your people are working at jobs unrelieved by events, you should think in terms of introducing some element of excitement into their working lives. Try, for instance, taking some of them to your next product launch.

3. Putting on uniform turned boring factory hands and farm boys into instant 'heroes' giving them RECOGNITION, APPROBATION and INCREASED STATUS, all of which are strong motivations.

    Managerial appreciation is extremely motivating, as is peer recognition and approval.

4. The army and navy offered the chance of travel – many of the volunteers had never been more than a mile or two from their homes – comradeship, challenge and a chance to try something new which would perhaps mean an OPPORTUNITY FOR ADVANCEMENT.

All these – even travel in the form of holidays and prizes – can be highly motivating for today's employees.

5. The volunteers had A DEFINITE GOAL i.e. to beat the Germans, and a DEADLINE – it would 'all be over by Christmas'.

Both of these factors have relevance today. It is motivating to have a specific goal and to know that you intend to reach it by a certain date.

6. Potential volunteers were the targets for much astute 'ADVERTISING AND PR' – often incorporating humour – together with a great deal of what came to be called propaganda.

We can deplore the lies and the cynicism – counterproductive in the long run – while noting the effective techniques which were used.

7. PEER PRESSURE. One example of this was the woman who distributed white feathers to men not in uniform. This was despicable – especially as many of the men concerned were on convalescent leave from the trenches – but it indicates how much people can be influenced by the opinions of others.

• By pointing out, for instance, that absenteeism and persistent lateness increases the work load for everyone you could turn most of your people into time watchdogs. This can be more effective than reporting offenders to management.

8. The soldiers were PROMISED that their jobs would be kept open and they would return to a land fit for heroes. In the event, there were bands of wounded, bemedalled ex-soldiers playing war-time hit songs as they begged in the street.

Managers should regard promises as powerful but potentially dangerous motivating factors. A PROMISE NOT KEPT has a −M value out of all proportion to the +M value of the original promise.

9. Soldiers were RELEASED FROM CONSTRAINTS AND TABOOS e.g. they were encouraged to break the sixth commandment.

An unlikely motivation in business life, but compare for example the Japanese motivation idea of releasing tension by physically assaulting a lifelike effigy of the boss.

A BIT OF STICK

Even when the volunteers began training there were still some 'carrot' factors in operation, although the 'stick' soon became more evident. Some of the carrot factors which persuaded people to join up, like comradeship and being part of something bigger than oneself i.e. the Regiment, were strengthened. Other factors were:

1. DISCIPLINE. Many soldiers found it motivating to have easily understood rules by which to order their activities and did not mind too much if these were imposed.

   You can give many of your people a genuine sense of security by defining the limits of the autonomy you are prepared to allow, the standards you intend to set and so on – in other words by structuring your motivation effort.

2. FITNESS. Most of the fatal casualties were fitter and more full of motivating energy when they died than they had ever been in their lives and physical fitness is still an important if neglected motivator.

   Take an interest – active if possible – in your company's sporting activities and first aid training.

3. FEAR – Fear of punishment, including that of being shot by their own side, but – more importantly for us – FEAR OF CENSURE by superiors and equals.

   Fear of censure is still legitimate motivation but managerial criticism should be private and constructive.

4. MEDALS and promotions.

   RECOGNITION and the POSSIBILITY OF ADVANCEMENT

are still important motivators. You should make sure all of your people have a chance to develop their potential.

5. LEADERSHIP. Some of the top brass were completely inadequate: a German general described the British troops as 'lions led by donkeys', but the leadership of many of the more junior officers and non-commissioned officers was beyond praise.

It has taken a long time for the idea of the motivating effect of good middle management to filter through to industry, but leadership is now regarded as an important M factor at all levels.

TWENTY YEARS ON

By 1939 and the outbreak of the Second World War the services, having learned very little from the First, had gone back to peacetime soldiering, offering a haven for the unemployed in the ranks and a gentlemen's club for the officers.

From the beginning of the fighting an almost unrelieved series of disasters, lasting more than two years, eventually caused some politicians and Service Chiefs to consider that they might not have been supplying the fighting men with the right motivation, the right means or the right opportunities.

Suddenly, they realised that the WHO? they needed to motivate had changed yet again and, although flag waving patriots by today's standards, the civilian soldiers were not only literate, comparatively well informed, thoughtful and innovative but were prepared to ask 'the reason why' they were being asked to do or die.

THE ARMY MOVES INTO THE MOTIVATION BUSINESS

Overnight the Army discovered motivating concepts like INVOLVEMENT, COMMUNICATION, and the exploitation of human potential by promotion from the ranks.

THE HORSE AND BUGGY MOTIVATION OF INDUSTRY

On the 'Home Front' a combination of Jingoism, genuine patriotism and a desire for revenge, together with high wages, had kept industry motivated during the war, though not as effectively as the propaganda of the day had people believe.

With the coming of peace in 1945, industry largely returned to the familiar adversarial pattern and the carrot and stick motivating methods of the past. In many cases even the unions saw money as the only motivation and 'shorter hours' often meant 'more overtime'.

To be fair, most people were too exhausted to be motivated; they were forced to work with old, worn out equipment, were led by tired and used up management and, more importantly, they were without the sense of purpose which had motivated their wartime sacrifices. 'Enjoy the war – the peace will be terrible' was a German wartime saying that seemed to have come true for the victors as well as the vanquished.

THE BOYS COME MARCHING HOME

Back into this grey unmotivated world came the ex-servicemen in their hundreds of thousands – not professional soldiers, sailors or airmen but civilians of all classes and grades who had travelled the world, some of them for years, accepting life and death responsibility, forming teams, solving problems, demanding to be informed.

Many of them had become highly experienced managers, completely different from when they joined up and totally different from those managers who had remained behind.

THE NEW MIDDLE MANAGEMENT

After the Second World War – by contrast with the first – the majority of the bright young leaders had not been killed off.

Of course some ex-Army 'managers' found the office boy sitting in their chair when they returned, but very slowly, and against great opposition, they began to introduce the motivating style of leadership they had learned the hard way.

At the same time the younger professionals who remained in the services slowly began working their way up to positions of influence. By the 1960s and 70s they would have a tremendous influence on the training and motivation of leaders for business and industry.

Enter the Gurus

Meanwhile motivation had become the subject of much academic research and speculation and some of the leading behavioural psychologists of the day were writing about how managers could motivate their individual employees, groups and companies.

Many of them merely re-stated the problems but others attempted to provide solutions to real life situations and it was these who would eventually influence progressive managers and achieve guru status.

Managers can still learn a great deal from the early gurus but it is essential to remember that, although the problems they addressed were similar to those facing managers today, the WHO? has changed even in the last couple of decades. Today's employees are not the same WHO? as their fathers were and do not respond to precisely the same motivation.

However, having looked at what motivated people in the past and the factors that still motivate them, we can now examine the work of the gurus, who fed the new managers' appetite for motivating ideas and their demand for practical advice – and in fact began what now bids fair to become a motivational revolution.

Summary

- Managers, who need only to motivate people to give of their best in the workplace, can learn from the ways in which men have been motivated to risk their lives. At first these were mainly 'stick' factors but later, most men fought for glory, pay and the chance of booty.

- The First World War saw the end of money as a motivating factor for most armies. Non-financial motivating factors took the place of money. Motivators were often cynical manipulators but their motivating achievements, though tragic in their consequences, were astonishing.
- By the time of the Second World War the WHO? that needed to be motivated had changed yet again and new motivations had to be employed. Together, returning professional soldiers and demobilised 'civilian' soldiers would change the motivation of business – but it would take time.
- The need for new motivation to overcome post-war apathy stimulated interest in the motivation 'gurus' whose work encouraged the new managers to undertake successful experiments resulting in the current trend towards a return to the Pleasure Principle.

ACTION

- List those factors which motivated World War I soldiers and which still motivate a) today b) in your operation.
- Read at least a portion of any book dealing with front line operations in World War I to discover what motivated human beings are capable of.

6. There's No Such Thing As a Bad Guru

You can fly the Atlantic in Concorde, travelling 12 miles high at the speed of a rifle bullet, without knowing how the machine works. Given adequate training, you could even fly the plane, without knowing much about its design, its construction or the theory of jet propulsion as applied to heavier than air flight.

What pilots need to know is how to fly, which can best be learned by flying everything from gliders to Jumbos before moving on to Concorde, at which stage the finest teachers are going to be experienced Concorde pilots.

For the pilot the problem – getting off the ground, staying in the air and coming safely down again – is the same as that which confronted the Wright brothers; only the WHAT? of the machine he flies has changed. In the same way, what managers need to know about the business of motivation is how to motivate business – which involves motivating people to do specific things like working in factories, and hunting for sales.

WHY BOTHER WITH THEORY?

Some of the highly successful managers we talked to when researching this book had barely heard of most of the theorists, although they were obviously using methods related to their work. So why bother with theory? Knowing a few heavy names is an amusing bit of one upmanship – "What! You mean to say you have never heard of Herzberg?" – which is not very helpful.

What managers will find useful is to examine the work of those academics who have taken a long hard look at the sharp end of management, all of whom have some useable ideas, and one or two of whom are outstanding. In fact, there is no such thing as a bad guru as there is something to be learned from all of them.

TAYLORISM AND THE MOTIVATION OF HOMUS ECONOMICUS

American Quaker Frederick Winslow Taylor – who may sound vaguely familiar to anyone old enough to have seen the movie *'Cheaper by the Dozen'* – was the practice oriented guru par excellence. He began as a labourer with the Midvale Steel Works and worked his way up to chief engineer, before moving to Bethlehem Steel in Pittsburg as consulting engineer in management, where he became the father of 'time and motion study'.

His motivation ideas were based largely on financial incentives and his most famous example was a labourer at Bethlehem who increased his daily 'tonnage handled' from 16 tons to 49 when his wages were upped from 1.15 dollars to 1.88 dollars.

Taylor died in 1917 so the stakhanovite of Bethlehem Steel almost certainly differed in culture from the WHO? managers need to motivate today. However, Taylor's conviction that 'the principal object of management should be to secure the maximum prosperity for the employer, coupled with the maximum prosperity of each employee' was a motivational breakthrough, as were his views on middle management responsibilities, the co-operation of workers and management, and his institution of rudimentary quality circles.

THEORY X AND THEORY Y

Theory X (authoritarian management) and 'Theory Y' (management by participation) were put forward in 1960 by American psychologist Douglas McGregor in his book *The Human Side of Enterprise*.

THE ABRAHAM MASLOW **'HIERARCHY OF NEEDS'** PYRAMID

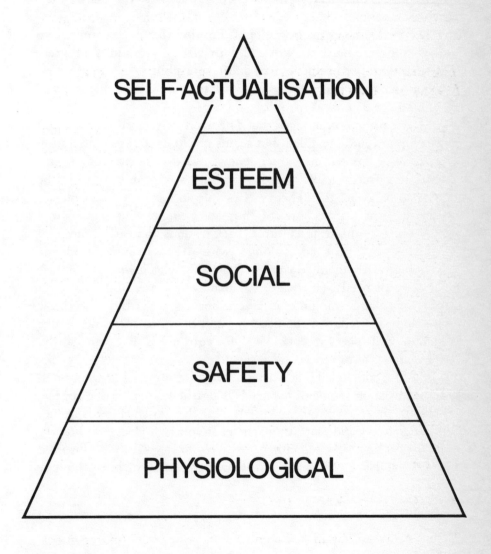

SELF-ACTUALISATION

ESTEEM

SOCIAL

SAFETY

PHYSIOLOGICAL

As a Bad Guru

... that most people are lazy, hate work, are
... onsibility and will only work if motivated by
... actors.

... days when they are convinced that, with the
... lves, the world is populated exclusively by
Theory X ...

Theory Y makes the opposite assumption that most people have a psychological need to work and that they are adults of great potential who need achievement and responsibility.

Fortunate managers have days when they are certain that some of their staff are Theory Y people.

McGregor was convinced that Theory X originated with the end of the hunter-gatherer Eden, but seems not to have appreciated fully that the logical outcome of a tendency towards Theory Y is a return to the Pleasure Principle and the exciting work game. Nor did he appear to be aware that Theory X people and Theory Y people are essentially the same sort of human beings who have been conditioned by differing cultures, backgrounds and early training.

McGregor believed, along with the mainly academic psychologist Abraham Maslow (1908-1970) who coined the phrase 'hierarchy of needs' (see page 33), that people are motivated by a series of wants ranging in ascending order from the basic physiological needs via the need for security – to social needs like affection and peer acceptance – to ego needs like autonomy, achievement, recognition and respect.

Maslow concluded that Man is a 'wanting animal' but went on to say that 'as soon as one of his needs is satisfied, another one appears to take its place', without making it clear that satisfied needs do not simply go away and that, for instance, anyone who has gone hungry will always be motivated either positively or negatively by his need for food and the possibility – however remote – of being hungry again.

The Six Assumptions for Theory Y

McGregor's six assumptions for Theory Y were:

1. that the average human being does not dislike work and that work could be enjoyable depending on controllable conditions;

2. that people will exercise self-direction and self-control if they are committed to an objective;

3. that commitment to objectives is a function of the rewards associated with their achievement, the most significant of which are ego satisfactions like recognition;

4. that, given the proper conditions, the average human being will not only accept but will seek responsibility;

5. that most people have a high potential;

6. that this potential was being only partially utilised.

Maslow's Self-Actualising 'Mensch'

In addition to the 'hierarchy of needs', Professor Maslow's other important contribution to motivation was his concept of the 'self-actualising man' which he put forward in 1950 in a paper 'Self-Actualising People: A Study of Psychological Health'.

Self-actualising people, he asserted, are good judges of character, enjoy intellectual challenge, accept all human frailties including their own as 'natural', are spontaneous, extrovert, detached, independent, young in heart and have a genuine desire to help the human race. They are true democrats with an 'unhostile' sense of humour who respect and are willing to be friendly with anybody and are prepared to question cultural values.

Maslow, who instanced examples like Lincoln, Spinoza and Eleanor Roosevelt, asserted that self-actualising people are an elite of character, capacity and talent rather than birth, fame or power. His psychologically healthy person comes very close to the Holistic Winners we have described elsewhere as being 'happy in their skin'. In fact, everyone is capable of some degree of self-actualisation and most of us are capable of improvement.

Motivating people by helping them to become self-actualising 'winners' is something today's successful managers regard as an important part of their motivation strategy.

THE WEAKNESS OF THEORY 'Y'

Maslow criticised Theory 'Y' because even strong, mature people need the security of some degree of guidance, and also because it would ask too much of those individuals who could not take the burden of responsibility. In practice, managers find that even strong people who are thrown in at the deep end need to know there is help available, and that some people are so culturally set in their ways as to make Theory 'Y' motivation difficult.

However, there are people like the hospital porter of our Worthing case study (see Chapter 16) who became an ideas dynamo at the first hint of 'involvement', which suggests that, while no one should be made to feel uncomfortable, everyone should be given the opportunity to become involved, even if the involvement is minimal to begin with.

People are almost always a lot brighter than their bosses believe.

WORKERS ARE PEOPLE

Elton W. Mayo led the famous Hawthorne Experiments at Western Electric's Hawthorne Works in Chicago from 1927 to 1932. The experiments, which continued until 1937, were conducted by a Harvard supervised team of around 100 investigators working with 20,000 employees.

Mayo used test groups, each consisting of six women, and after discussing his plans with the groups made as many as ten improvements in their working conditions.

Understandably, output increased each time a change was put into effect, but the big surprise came when the workers were asked to go back to the old conditions with, for example, no rest breaks and no incentives.

OUTPUT ROSE AGAIN TO THE HIGHEST THE PLANT HAD SEEN and absenteeism went down by 80 per cent.

Mayo concluded that the workers had been motivated simply by being NOTICED and CONSULTED and that the increase in their SELF-ESTEEM was even more important to them than improvements in working conditions or increased wages.

The discovery that workers are adult human beings who respond well to being treated as adult human beings was, in its day, a breach in the wall between 'them' and 'us'. Mayo had seriously dented Taylorism with its accent on financial rewards and had demonstrated the need for communication between management and the managed.

HERZBERG AND HYGIENE

Frederick Herzberg, born in 1923, is the American clinical psychologist and professor of management who separated the elements of a job into those serving animal or economic needs, which he called 'hygiene' or 'maintenance' factors, and those meeting deeper aspirations, like the desire for achievement or recognition, which he called 'motivation' factors.

Herzberg, who came up with the idea that jobs could be 'enriched' by adding motivation factors – thus in his words 'giving employment to a hell of a lot of consultants' – believed that Man has two sets of needs: 'his needs as an animal to avoid pain and his need as a human to grow psychologically'.

This is a handy way of expressing the fact that (in varying degrees) people can be motivated by the crudest of sticks and also by the most sophisticated of carrots. Herzberg asserted that it was his 'motivation' factors which led to a feeling of satisfaction i.e. factors like achievement, recognition, satisfaction in the nature of the work itself, responsibility, progress and personal growth, while dissatisfaction always related to hygiene factors like company policy, working conditions, salary, status and job security.

It is perhaps simpler to consider all these factors and many others as 'M', or motivating factors, which can be quantified in any given situation as either +M or –M depending on the Who?, What?, When?, Where? and Why?

Salary, company policy and working conditions for example can be +M i.e. intensely satisfying and motivating in the desired direction, while achievement and recognition, if not present to a satisfactory degree, can be –M, i.e. exactly the opposite.

COMMON SENSE IN THE SIXTIES

Herzberg's summary of his thoughts on motivation, published in 1968 as an article in the Harvard Business Review, sold well over a million reprinted copies.

This is because he was not just a theoretician but had worked in industry, as a consultant for AT & T Telecommunications. He addressed managers' motivation problems head on and used some down to earth expressions which made managers feel he was not just an ivory tower academic.

More importantly, he put into words the growing feeling of America's middle managers of the late 60s that they wanted more from their own jobs than money and status and the view of many of America's senior managers that they would look with favour on any motivation plan that wasn't going to cost a lot of money. It is worth bearing in mind that at the time some big American companies were motivating not just by salary but by 'sumptuary laws', which laid down, for example, what sort of houses employees of a particular grade would occupy, what type and size of cars they would drive and how many hours of home help they would employ, before graduating to a full time domestic. Giving salesmen's wives one earring so they would motivate their husbands to earn the second was standard motivation practice. In this climate Herzberg came as a breath of common sense and was hailed accordingly.

Motivating by Kita

Herzberg's opening sentence went straight to the heart of the problem with the question everyone was asking – 'How do I get an employee to do what I want?'

His first reply was that 'the simplest, surest and most direct way' was 'Ask them', and this is a valid answer which we shall be expanding. However, if the person in question didn't want to do it, your choices, said Herzberg, included a psychological consultation to find out the reason for such obduracy, a communications expert to tell you how to get through to him, a money incentive or a costly training programme.

We need a simple way, said Herzberg, and the simplest and most direct way would be a Kick In The Ass or what he called a negative physical KITA.

This approach, though tempting in some ways, had drawbacks, not the least of which was the risk of being kicked back, while negative psychological KITA or ego bashing did not motivate.

Herzberg then went on to address – with telling sarcasm – what he called 'The myths of motivation', describing for instance the reduction of hours as 'a marvellous way of motivating people – getting them off the job'.

In the same way he dealt with wage increases, fringe benefits, human relations, sensitivity training, communications, two-way communications, job participation and employee counselling.

Job Enrichment

The professor then detailed his ideas on job enrichment, including what now seems contradictory advice to 'avoid all direct participation by the employees whose jobs are to be enriched'.

He also cited a study in which jobs had been enriched by for example having correspondents sign their own names to letters instead of their being signed by the supervisor, encouraging correspondents to write in a more personalised way instead of sending form letters, and cutting verification by supervisors from 100 per cent to 10 per cent of all letters.

Herzberg's ideas about job enrichment proved of great value in practice, but his insistence on the dichotomy between hygiene and motivation factors called for some pretty fancy footwork from his uncritical supporters when workers insisted that they were motiviated by hygiene factors like money.

THERE IS LIFE AFTER HERZBERG

Rosabeth Moss Kanter, professor of Business Administration at Harvard, editor of the *Harvard Business Review*, and the author of an impressive trilogy of books: *Men and Women of the Corporation* (1977), *The Change Masters* (1983) and *When Giants Learn to Dance* (1989), identifies empowerment as a key motivational factor and suggests that management should be opened up to promotion from the ranks of the powerless – like women and clerical workers. She also advocates decentralised authority and autonomous work groups to help achieve synergy. She identifies the factors which create power or powerlessness (make power a +M or −M factor) as discretion, recognition, relevance to central problems, peer networks and subordinates. She asserts that by empowering others leaders do not decrease their power and can INCREASE it if the whole organisation improves its performance as a result. Her seven essential skills for managers of the future include motivating factors like being able to gain satisfaction from results and being willing to stake one's own rewards on them, a dose of humility in the sense of not being a know-all, and operating to high ethical standards.

VROOM, VROOM

Apart from having a splendid name for a motivation expert Victor Vroom, by looking at motivation from the angle of the motivee, has arrived at ideas which appeal to those who combine theory and practice – like Claude Lambshead who teaches marketing and management at the University of Bristol and specialises in helping people set up small businesses. Says Lambshead, 'Vroom maintains that people ask themselves three questions before they are in a motivated state: 1) Can I do what I am being asked to do? 2) Would I be rewarded for doing it? 3) Do I want the reward on offer?

'If I ask a subordinate to do something, the first thing he is going to ask himself is whether, if he tries, his efforts are likely to produce results. If he does try, and the answer is no, he will be demotivated. Perhaps this implies that the individual needs training or a change of attitude.

'The problem with the second of Vroom's criteria is that in many organisations the rewards for specific tasks are very unspecific and an atmosphere is created where people don't believe they will be rewarded. 'Often the boss says they will be rewarded but it never really happens – as when a manager says something like "If you keep up this performance, you've got a good future here." The boss instantly forgets his offhand remark but the promise is important to the subordinate who is very demotivated when, having kept up his performance, nothing happens.

'If the subordinate feels that he CAN do the job, and is confident that he WILL be rewarded, then his next question is whether he wants what the reward is. In many cases, for example, the reward on offer is a promotion and plenty of managers are not turned on by the prospect of a further promotion which might mean a move, a change in life-style and more work.

'What tends to happen is that people in their twenties or thirties with kids and mortgages are still motivated by money, but for people in their forties there's a need for an idiosyncratic "cafeteria" approach in which people choose their own motivational package.'

There's evidence that self-actualisation, especially that resulting from a degree of autonomy, plays an increasingly large part in the motivation package older people are looking for. 'We get people of 30 and 40 who want to set up small businesses even though economically it doesn't make sense because they'll never make the money they are getting with the big corporations. They want to do their own thing because they don't want to be told what to do; they are interested in self-actualisation and have a high need for autonomy.'

Moral: IF YOU WANT TO MOTIVATE AND RETAIN YOUR 'FORTY SOMETHING' PEOPLE – EMPOWER THEM.

LEADERSHIP AS A MOTIVATOR

Cambridge graduate, ex-Guards Officer and qualified Icelandic trawler 'decky' John Adair has developed the concept of Action-Centred Leadership and argues that leadership is all about inspiring others by means of one's own enthusiasm, commitment and the ability to communicate enthusiasm to other people.

Stressing the need for teamwork, and for leaders to create teams, Adair's Action-Centred Learning model of three overlapping circles emphasises his belief that working groups share three needs: the need to accomplish a common task, the need to be maintained as a team and the sum of the group's individual needs – and that failure in one area affects the other two.

Most motivation specialists believe with Adair that leadership is of paramount importance both at the strategic and tactical levels because of the high M levels, both plus and minus, that it can generate and that, whatever structure an organisation adopts, leadership will remain one of the most important single motivating factors.

MOTIVATION AT DIFFERENT LEVELS

In his excellent book 'The Action-Centred Leader' John Adair makes the important point that your approach to motivation can vary depending upon where you, and the people you wish to motivate, are within an organisation. The WHO? will vary enormously from organisation to organisation and within specific organisations, suggesting that in most cases structured management is called for.

TOM PETERS AND THE CULT OF EXCELLENCE

Excellence is a 'noble cause' motivation, which perhaps explains why Tom Peters' 'In Search of Excellence' became the world's best selling business book. Later, in '*Thriving on Chaos*' he propounded 45 rules for managers at every level, including such powerful motivating factors as: making front line people 'company heroes', applauding champions, involvement, quality, core values (another worthwhile cause) and leadership by personal example.

SUMMARY

- All managers, theorists and gurus are looking at the same problem in different ways: Herzberg's 'How do I get an employee to do what I want?'
- Over the years, employees – i.e. the WHO? of motivation – have changed with their changing culture and most theorists have responded with an increasingly humanist, Pleasure Principle approach.
- The theorists have changed and are changing with the WHO? from Taylorism to Tom Peters.
- There is no such thing as a bad guru. We can learn something from all of them, even if it is only to watch our blood pressure.
- Many theorists appear to adopt a stretch-and-trim approach to data which seems to contradict their ideas, indicating that they are as human in their motivation as the rest of us.
- Managers should innovate with caution. Practical sense and practice-based theoretical work like Vroom's employee-oriented approach can provide useful ideas.

ACTION

- Get hold of a book by a guru you agree with and another whose ideas do not appeal to you. Follow up the ideas that interest you most and are most relevant to your situation and that of your organisation.

7. The Leadership Factor

All managers are leaders, if only by virtue of their managerial status, but in today's highly competitive world the title is not enough and, if you are to motivate your troops, you need to be both an example and an inspiration.

Fortunately, leadership is one aspect of motivation which you can control. For example, depending on the degree of autonomy you enjoy, it is you who control your management style and you who decide whether you rule by fear or by consensus. Even in companies where a house management style is imposed, or understood, the scope for individual managers to develop a personal style is enormous. You are very much in control and if your current method of leadership is not motivating the people who report to you, you can change it.

As a manager you may also have control over the people you need to lead. You should be in a position to hire the best, train the rest and get rid of the pest. In other words, you control both the leadership and the composition of the led, so if your people are unmotivated and useless, there is no prize for guessing who is to blame.

Once you have got rid of the deadlegs that you either inherited or hired by mistake there really is no such thing as a bad employee – only a bad manager.

WANTED – MORE LEADERSHIP

Leadership has an extremely high M factor in that good leadership is highly motivating while bad leadership is exactly the opposite. This is the case in the world of business, whether your organisation employs half a dozen people or is a multi-national corporation. The fact that the most highly motivated modern businesses are empowering their people – some to the point of creating virtually autonomous businesses within the organisation – does not imply that top management has abdicated its responsibilities. What it does mean is that top management is freed to get on with its task of planning strategies, middle managers can get on with the job of managing their section of the enterprise and supervisors can coach their teams to the point where they can make many of their own decisions without having to refer upwards, especially in those areas which they know better than anyone else.

In today's motivation conscious enterprise, top management expects many decisions to be taken by the people who will be most affected by them, and who are close enough to the problems for the answers to matter both to them and to the people who are their internal or external customers.

MORE LEADERS MEANS BETTER MOTIVATION

If it is to succeed, the business of today needs not less leadership but more leadership. In fact, the whole organisation must be permeated by leadership from the boardroom right down to shop floors and offices, but where are these new leaders to come from?

The answer is that if you have faith in yourself as a leader, and are happy with your style, you can teach your people to become leaders by giving them the opportunity to lead, while at the same time letting them know you have confidence in their ability and that you will be available to help them should they make mistakes. Empowerment will allow you to harness the abilities and the motivating force of the entire workforce, but at each level someone has to make the decisions.

Policy decisions, for example, are made by policy making leaders and in the case of the well motivated organisations we studied, every one had a highly visible leader who had taken a conscious decision to motivate and to involve his, or her, people in the decision making process.

MOTIVATING LEADERS TO MOTIVATE

One large organisation which has to be ready to face more serious problems than most, and whose motivation specialists are held in high esteem by industry, is the British Army.

As the Army's Director General of Training, Major General S. C. Grant is responsible for producing the leaders who will motivate an organisation employing 116,000 people.

Scott Grant, who joined the Army as a Sandhurst cadet at 19 and is a Royal Engineers officer with an 'in service' Cambridge degree, has seen active service in the Persian Gulf, Germany and Northern Ireland and has commanded both a Squadron and a Brigade. Underlining the fact that the Army never stops training, in addition to spending two years as an instructor at Sandhurst, General Grant spent two years at Staff College undergoing technical training and General Staff training, and recently spent a year at the Royal College of Defence Studies.

His endorsement of the importance of motivation is unequivocal. 'Man is not a finite resource. If he is well motivated a man can achieve a great deal, but if he's badly motivated he won't achieve anything and this becomes apparent to an army officer at quite an early stage in his career.'

THE SELF-ACTUALISING SOLDIER

'The most important thing,' emphasises General Grant, 'is the soldier's belief in himself, and for any commander – as for any motivator – the secret is to build up the man's self-esteem, to create an image of himself which he must adhere to, and to set standards he feels he must meet. You must make the individual feel that he is important – someone special.

'Regimental insignia, medals, red berets and so on create the belief in the soldier that he is part of an elite and that he must aim for the standards of the elite. This is probably more difficult in civilian life where you do not have physical manifestations of promotions or awards. We have high standards, a regimental system which bonds people closely together, camaraderie and A BELIEF THAT WHAT WE ARE DOING IS IMPORTANT. If you believe in the job you are doing, and in the people with whom you are doing the job, they become totally loyal to you and you become totally committed to them and this is what drives you.'

- Are you building up the self-esteem of your own 'troops' or are you using psychological KITA to bring them to heel?
- You should encourage your people to believe they are members of an elite. 'Physical manifestations of promotions or awards', if you use them as motivations, should be seen by everyone to have been earned.
- As a manager, you must set high standards both for yourself and for the people who report to you, and convince them that what they are doing is important; for you, for them, for the organisation and for their internal and external customers.

THE BENEFITS OF THE HIERARCHY

In a world in which management hierarchies are being changed and dismantled, the Army remains a highly structured organisation, but General Grant sees motivating advantages in this.

'We are driven to it by what, in managerial terms, would be described as our output, which requires individuals to carry out activities in conditions of extreme danger and to implement orders without discussion, and so to some extent we must build an organisation which leads to obedience.

'However, strangely enough, the formalised hierarchy makes for a great freedom of expression, because there is no requirement for people to assert their personal position as the hierarchy has already been established.

'In civilian organisations a great deal of time is spent initially on establishing position. In the Army, no time is wasted on this sort of jockeying and people can express their views, make a contribution and participate in debate, in the full knowledge that AT THE END OF THE DAY THE CHAP WHO CARRIES THE RANK MUST MAKE THE DECISION. This means there is a freer exchange of views prior to the decision and that in the end the decision is better based and is more likely to be accepted by those taking part in the process.

'It's not a formalised system; it's something all commanders learn with experience, namely that there is information available within the corporate body and that you must take advantage of it. Everyone has an interest in making a good decision but I would stress that the responsibility for making the decision remains that of the commander.'

- Managers should consider this extremely motivating style of leadership (a) for the people who report to them i.e. their own 'team' and (b) for any teams they set up. The maximum number for leadership-based discussions of this sort in which all the team participate – followed by a firm understanding that no more discussion is allowed – is around a dozen. When it works well the system can work miracles.

WHEN 'THEM' AND 'US' BECOMES "WE"

It would be quite wrong, General Grant insisted, to believe that because the Army has a hierarchy this in any way excludes one part of the organisation from another. 'You are a soldier twenty four hours a day. There is no equivalent of the civilian managing director coming out of his factory and turning one way while his workers turn the other. We live together and we are all of the same body.'

The Army has an obvious 'them' and an equally obvious 'us', but in good units these – although imposed and traditional – are transcended by the 'we'.

In many civilian organisations the differences are equally great and are resented rather than accepted, which is immensely demotivating. The managers' job is to minimise demotivation by demonstrating that: in their organisation 'them' and 'us' pettiness no longer exists, i.e. their outfit is not 'class-ridden', that training and educational opportunities have rendered the boundaries more fluid and that the 'we' are in fact 'members of the same body'.

'SHOP FLOOR' INITIATIVE

'The British Army,' the General made clear, 'relies on quite junior ranks to exercise initiative, within the guidelines laid down by the overall commander.

'If you take a situation like Northern Ireland, you may have a patrol of very few soldiers, and it is up to those soldiers to make decisions, within the guidelines they have been given and according to the training they have had prior to deploying. They clearly have communications which enable them to seek advice in extremis, but we train people to make decisions and we set standards that I hope mean that they will make the right decisions.'

Let your people in the front line make decisions, train them to make the right ones and let them know that you are there to provide backing and help if needed. If you can convince them that you will carry the can for any decisions made within your guidelines that turn out to be wrong – so much the better.

NO WASTE OF HUMAN RESOURCES

The Army's method of making the optimum use of human resources is clearly pragmatic.

Soldiers who enter as Privates, Sappers or Gunners, says General Grant, have 'a real possibility of being commissioned and of reaching the rank of Lt. Colonel Quartermaster.

'That is one way forward. Another is that if a soldier, on entering, shows unusual ability, he can be pulled out, can hone up his educational skills, go to a Regular Commission Board and then to Sandhurst. He is then a Regular Officer like everyone else and as such could become a Field Marshal.

'When I was a Commanding Officer, for example, I was succeeded by a chap who had reached the rank of Corporal when someone recognised his ability and decided he should be commissioned.'

Potential high flyers should be recruited as such or identified as soon as possible after joining your organisation.

Make sure every one knows what career paths exist and where they can lead to, especially if there is a ceiling. Clearly, knowing that opportunities exist is motivating. On the other hand, it is the job of the manager to make sure that people are on – or can move to – a career path that suits THEM, not the company, and that there is no danger of people being demotivated, as von Clausewitz put it, by 'losing their energy on being raised to a higher position to which they do not feel themselves equal'.

CHALLENGES AND ENJOYMENT

The great enjoyments of life, said General Grant, are achieved by 'being set difficult tasks and overcoming them', adding that to demand high standards of people is to express confidence in their abilities, while expecting low standards is a vote of no confidence. He might have added that it is also a self-fulfilling prophecy.

HOW THE CAPTAINS AND MAJORS BECAME CAPTAINS OF INDUSTRY

'The Leaders of Industry,' wrote Carlyle in 1843, 'are virtually Captains of the World', but for the captains he was speaking about – with rare exceptions including Quaker families like the Cadburys and the Frys – their 'soldiers', as poet Louis MacNeice would later put it, were 'cogs in a machine, a thing with one face.'

However, the WHO? was changing and leadership was being forced to change too. In France, mining engineer Henri Fayol had identified motivation, or 'getting the organisation going', as an important element of command, asserting among other things that managers should:

- set a good example;
- involve their chief assistants by means of conference;
- 'aim at making unity, energy, initiative and loyalty prevail amongst all employees.'

This was revolutionary stuff in 1916 and it was still new enough to be exciting when it appeared in translation in 1949 when the 'Management through Leadership' revolution – which had begun with the Army around 1944 – was under way.

CHOOSING LEADERS

As John Adair points out in *Great Leaders*, during World War II a working party of senior officers and psychologists, including the American social psychologist W. R. Bion, developed a new method of selecting leaders called the War Office Selection Board (WOSB) which was the forerunner of today's assessment centres.

These WOSBs, usually held in large country houses, lasted several days. Candidates were placed in groups which were given tasks to perform – like building bridges over streams or getting barrels across them, all with very little equipment.

Candidates were put under stress and the selectors watched the 'command tasks' to see how far each individual candidate helped the group achieve its tasks and maintain its cohesion as a team. Later, when Adair lectured at Sandhurst, he would develop this idea, exemplified by the three overlapping circles, as Action-Centred Leadership.

Strangely, most of industry has only recently begun to exploit the assessment centre, although very soon after World War II the more go-ahead companies began to adopt some of the motivating methods of the victorious 'citizens' army'.

MOTIVATING A CLASSIC TURN ROUND

If you are faced with the job of turning round an unmotivated and demoralised company or department you face a bigger challenge than that involved in improving the motivation of an organisation which is already doing reasonably well. The advantage is that your results will be highly visible and almost certainly quantifiable.

On 13 August 1942, for example, when Montgomery arrived to take command of the defeated and broken Eighth Army two months before the battle of El Alamein, the atmosphere, as he wrote in his diary, was 'dismal and dreary'.

Realising that motivation stems from the top, he spoke that evening to the 50 to 60 strong staff of Eighth Army H.Q. and told them, using many easily recognisable motivating factors, that:

1. They had got to work together; therefore they must understand each other and have confidence in one another.

2. He had confidence in them. 'We will work together as a team and together we will gain the confidence of this great army and go forward to final victory in Africa.'

3. He did not like the defeatist 'atmosphere' in which planning for withdrawal was sapping confidence. 'We will stand and fight here.'

4. He told them the bad times were over and that the means – fresh divisions and Sherman tanks – had arrived.

5. He told them that they had a job to do and that it would be done. 'If anyone thinks it can't be done, let him go at once; I don't want any doubters in this party'.

6. The new atmosphere should permeate right down through the Eighth Army to the most junior private soldier.

7. He concluded, 'We are going to finish with this chap Rommel

once and for all. It will all be quite easy. There is no doubt about it. He is definitely a nuisance. Therefore we will hit him a crack and finish with him.'

Two months later the Eighth Army smashed Rommel and in doing so motivated Allied troops and civilians throughout the world by showing them they could win.

As Major General Grant put it 50 years later: 'People are motivated by word of mouth and by example, by contact with their superiors and by being inspired by them.'

MOTIVATING INDUSTRY

Enlightened self-interest and the need to win the war dictated the motivating leadership methods employed by Generals like Slim – 'No bad soldiers – only bad officers' – and Montgomery. When the war ended thousands of officers returned to their old jobs convinced that, as Vic Feather, General Secretary of the Trades Union Congress in the 1960s, put it, 'What industry needs now is not bosses but leaders.'

LEARN, ADAPT, IMPROVE

Industry is not the Army; shop floor and office workers are not soldiers; but industry could – and still can – learn from the Army, adapt the Army's motivation and leadership techniques to specific circumstances and improve them to motivate the increasingly better educated, better informed and more satisfaction conscious WHO? that is manning today's businesses.

In fact, some of the Army's top motivation experts are now counselling industry and their experience shows that Scott Grant's ideas on 'challenge, satisfaction and fun' are as valid outside the Army as in, and that, what he describes as the 'noble cause' could be the most important single element in the motivation of the young people who are the leaders of tomorrow.

Summary

- How management motivates a big organisation which makes extraordinary life and death demands on its people.
- The case for structure. The positive side of the hierarchy in saving time and encouraging participation.
- Choosing leaders to motivate. The importance of career paths, and opportunities to change direction.
- Desert Victory. How motivation can turn a situation round from failure to success.
- The M power of a NOBLE CAUSE.

Action

- Identify all the motivating factors mentioned above and take note of the ones you are already using. Decide if there are others you could use to good effect or whether you need to change the whole thrust of your motivation effort.

8. A Noble Cause

One man who proved to industry how the concept of Action Centred Leadership could be applied to the training of managers, is Colonel Blashford-Snell who commanded Sandhurst's Adventurous Training Wing, before founding the Exploration Society, and is now a consultant to the Ministry of Defence.

John Blashford-Snell, who knows as much about the practical motivation of individuals and groups as anyone alive, talked to us as he was preparing to lead a hundred strong expedition of doctors, managers and potential managers to Outer Mongolia.

Their three months' mission would take them to the Gobi Desert where they were to carry out eye operations and innoculate children against TB. It was a telling application of Scott Grant's 'noble cause' motivation to civilian life.

ORGANISING MOTIVATION

Blashford-Snell recalled how at Sandhurst in the 1960s he had been briefed by the Commandant, General Mogg – 'a highly motivated gentleman' who joined the Army as a soldier and, after being a Corporal, had gone to Sandhurst where he won the Sword of Honour and finished up as Deputy Commander Europe.

Until then Adventurous Training had been left to individual Commanding Officers who gave people unpaid leave to 'climb the Matterhorn' but now it was to be put on an organised footing as part of the individual's Army duty.

'What we were trying to do was to motivate people and give them confidence. We launched expeditions all over the world and sent them anywhere where they could do some good.

'They came back motivated and that helped to cut down the wastage that is bound to happen at a place like Sandhurst.'

Managers have to organise this type of motivation i.e. provide the original impetus, if it is to be effective. They can then stand back and see how their people take over and run things.

Warriors Without a War

Said Blashford-Snell, 'Young people today want to be warriors without a war and because of this a great deal of the work they did as part of their Adventurous Training was designed to help people.

'I used to go round the world once a year asking about jobs that needed to be done, like building schools, bridges, clinics – even churches. We did thousands of jobs until the Empire began to contract, as a result of which we ran out of aircraft, the tax payer no longer paid for our work and we needed charitable status in order to raise funds.

'We formed a charity called the Exploration Society which led to the founding of Operation Drake and Operation Raleigh. Then more and more people became interested in the application of the lessons we had learned to creating motivated leaders for industry. Professor John Adair was much involved and we all had a hand in the construction of the present system.'

Involve to Solve

Involving to solve is a prime motivating factor. 'We actually set the task and let them get on with it; they have to plan it and then fund it.'

You don't have to send people to Outer Mongolia to gain the motivating effects of involvement. Set them a task in the workplace and let them get on with it, and, where appropriate, handle their own budget.

Executive Expeditions

John Blashford-Snell is now running Executive Expeditions to remotivate senior managers who were impressed by the results when they sent their people on Operation Raleigh. 'We've had a real cross section of people ranging from a 70 year old American Corporation Chairman and the Chairman of the Halifax Building Society to people in their twenties.'

Candidates for the executive expeditions are put through the same sort of assessment tests as the people taking part in Operation Raleigh, which includes things like camping out at night in midwinter and handling pythons or tarantulas – tests designed, as their originator put it, to put people under stress. 'The important thing is that you have got to know how they will get on when the going gets rough. In other words, before you can motivate, you have to be fairly certain of your material. There are some people who are difficult to motivate.'

Managers could find both outdoor and indoor assessment tests valuable as a means of finding out how good their people are under stress and how easy or difficult they are to motivate. Some companies are now sending their junior managers on war game exercises to assess their leadership potential.

Once you have done the assessment, if you are not in a position to hire the best, train the rest and get rid of the pest, in the words of Professor Herzberg, 'you have a motivation problem.'

Motivating Factors

Executive Expeditions last for ten weeks and combine adventure training with the most demanding relief and research work in distant places. Recent operations have included the building of a medical aid centre in the Solomon Islands, studying flora and fauna in remote regions of Papua New Guinea and building a bridge in Southern Chile.

Returning 'venturers' like R. J. Leggett, the Personnel Administration Manager of Marconi, say they have 'broadened their horizons' and are 'better motivated in the workplace.'

John Hunt, the 50 year old General Manager of Marks and Spencer's store in Belfast, joined a party of 27 business managers aged from 28 to 53, including a Wall Street banker and a Midland Bank Operations Manager, on an expedition to Nepal. After white water rafting and elephant transport they reached deep jungle where their tasks included collecting plant specimens, documenting wild life and searching for a rogue elephant. John concluded that the experience made him a better motivated manager. He also came back with a quality control observation that M & S 'St Michael' underpants are not proof against the mice of the Nepalese jungle.

Challenge and 'Real' Problems

Blashford-Snell identifies challenge as a leading motivating factor, along with team development, realisation of potential, development of new skills and coping with unfamiliar situations.

'Perhaps more importantly they are facing real problems and helping real people.'

Operation Raleigh helps executives learn team development as a means of problem solving and winning. For example, when a bridge building team in Peru, that had been living off the land because of a customs strike, learned that the strike was over, a Japanese member requested, 'Don't send up the supplies. We are enjoying the challenge.'

The Case of the Motivated American

When Terry Linahan from Wisconsin was in Papua New Guinea on Operation Drake he asked Blashford-Snell if he could borrow $100 to buy a tree, to help a small island where the people had no boats with which to get their goods to market.

Most of the old men who knew how to build boats had died and people were just sitting round feeling sorry for themselves. Said Terry, 'If I can buy a tree, I can find the last canoe builders, set up a canoe building school for the young people, remotivate the whole tribe and bring it back to life.'

Terry got his $100 and bought his tree, only to discover that wood had to be seasoned for two years. He was told that the team couldn't wait that long but that he would be helped to form and lead his own team when the wood was ready.

CHALLENGES

Terry now 'owned' the problem and this motivated him to raise £20,000 to fund his team before setting off once more for Papua New Guinea, where he found the government had turned communist and were ready to put every obstacle in the way of foreigners who wanted to build canoes.

When he finally reached the island there was only one old man left alive who knew anything about canoes, but eventually the old man trained some apprentices, the canoe business became a great success and the remotivated islanders began to live again.

THEY CAN'T ALL GO TO NEW GUINEA

You can't send all your people off to Papua New Guinea or there would be nobody left to run the store. Not only that, but because they have been left unmotivated – if not demotivated – in the past, the people who need motivating the most are at the bottom of the hierarchic heap, which means there are more of them.

Instead, have them do something to help old people. Get them to suggest a project, fund it and run it, while you join in the work and maybe help with transport or equipment.

Operations like Raleigh have identified a vast fund of good will – especially in young people – which if properly harnessed will teach your people to work as teams, identify potential leaders and back up your motivation effort.

As a manager, a large proportion of your motivation effort should be devoted to exploiting the rich vein of cussedness and determination which exists in us all. To get your people to use this intensely motivating power for you rather than against you, involve to solve, but above all – EMPHASISE THE CHALLENGE NOT THE CHORE!

COMMUNICATION AND INSPIRATION

One lesson to be learned from the executive expeditions, says Blashford-Snell, is the motivating effect of communication across the gaps of age and rank. Asked what benefit she had derived from an expedition, one 27 year old ICI junior manager said that without doubt it had been sitting round the camp fire talking informally to a company chairman who was twenty years older than she was and had vast experience of management.

At the same time 70 year old top managers learn to communicate with their juniors, all of which is in stark contrast to some 'real life' workplace situations where bosses especially seem reluctant even to meet the workers. Another lesson has been the extent to which example motivates. A nurse who took a party of blind people from Southampton to Mount Kilabalu in Malaysia found that many of them were depressed and apathetic. She selected the most demotivated of all to make the climb first and they were so excited about their achievement they went back and motivated the others.

Managers should bear in mind the simplified principles of motivating leadership which Blashford-Snell applies to executive training and which he propounded after discovering that Churchill had listed 12 qualities of leadership, Eisenhower 14 and Montgomery 20. 'I decided I would never remember them all and so worked out two which are really vital and they were: to be able to communicate and to be able to inspire.'

THE PILKINGTON EXPERIENCE

Many highly motivated companies have successfully adapted the civilian version of the WOSB model to their own use. At their Lakeside Management Centre near St Helens on Merseyside the giant Pilkington glass group have harvested a motivation bonus by grafting an assessment centre onto their development programme for junior managers.

As management training and development consultants at the Centre Ron Shuttleworth and Roy Prescott reported in *Personnel*

Management (November 1991), the plan was tested on the Centre's two week executive development course for newly appointed junior managers, most of them graduates in their late twenties, drawn from Pilkington Companies in the UK and overseas. The course includes a business simulation, a 48 hour outdoor exercise and classroom based practical sessions, and its keynotes are 'active involvement and considerable pressure'.

The aims were to improve the effectiveness of participants when they returned to the real work situation and to get better information about the potential of future managers.

How Motivation Can Solve Problems

One problem was the release of personal information and the solution was a 'contract' between participants and personnel directors. The company would use the personal skills and development plans created on the course but would give participants the right to withold any of the information from the company. This meant that if full reports and plans were to be provided the personnel directors had to win the participants' trust.

Trust as a Motivation

The 'contract' built up great trust and openness: no participant chose to withold information and in fact all were motivated to regard the report and plan as an opportunity to make the company better informed about their individual skills and aspirations.

Change the Name, Change the Game

To avoid the divisive and demotivating feeling of being 'assessment fodder' the event was called a 'development planning workshop'.

In addition, a collaborative method of assessment was used in which the participant was provided with frank, helpful feedback from 'coaches' – not assessors – immediately after each exercise.

The role of the coach is to promote objectivity and

understanding, together with 'a spirit of working together in partnership', and to increase this, later courses used previous participants as coaches.

Once they discover that they 'own' the process of gathering information about their skills, participants themselves extend the process beyond the workshop.

The Pilkington Solution

Shuttleworth and Prescott's list shows the demotivating factors which can cause such courses to fail and what to do about it.

WHY COURSES FAIL AND WHAT TO DO ABOUT IT

Potential cause of inaction	Pilkington solution
Personal development plan aims at the wrong things	Development priorities are identified through the systematic comparison of job requirements and personal skills.
Plan is woolly and vague	Participants are set clear, work-related 'learning targets' with quite specific objectives.
The plan 'costs too much'	We ask participants to design learning methods that cost little or nothing – most do well.
No time – too busy	We also ask participants to design methods which make direct and substantial contributions to their job and most do. People find time for things of immediate benefit.
Participants are unused to planning development	We train the coaches in development planning, give examples of good development plans and provide a comprehensive menu of development ideas. Above all, we provide a structured development

	planning process, plus lots of help as people work through it.
Badly organised plan	We provide some development planning rules, some guidance and the time to think things through. Most importantly, we provide some checking of the plan by coaches.
No support from manager	Following the workshop, each participant meets with his or her manager, plus a coach. That meeting adds the manager's views to the skills report and agrees a final draft of the development plan (major differences are surprisingly rare).
No support from company	Personnel directors meet participants before the course and after to discuss the report and plan.
No monitoring of actions or quality of outputs	We monitor results by means of a follow-up questionnaire, participants' review six months after the course, systematic feedback from personnel directors and presentations of results.

Summary

- Some jobs, like newspapers or television journalism, are centred mainly on their 'events' content, while others have a high routine content which managers can counter by courses, adventurous training and assessments.

Still other jobs are repetitive to a marked degree and need an injection of 'events' if workers are not to become demotivated and alienated. The workers holding such jobs tend to be numerous and low down in the hierarchy, and 'events' must be specially tailored to their interests and desires.

Motivation specialists can help, in addition to which many companies run adventurous training courses in relatively accessible spots like the closest mountain range. Unfortunately the people most in need of motivation are the least likely to volunteer for canoing or abseiling, while people who are highly motivated will find adventure for themselves, but Operation Raleigh has provided one answer.

- There is a rich vein of social conscience to be found among almost all of us but especially among young people who find a 'noble cause' motivating. This is apparent for example in the case of College 'Rags' – fund raising events which break the routine of study and usually motivate the release of an amount of concentrated effort, ingenuity and energy that would earn, if employed academically, doctorates all round.

- Many firms find that 'events' linked to worthwhile causes are highly motivating morale boosters, especially if senior management is seen to be participating with enthusiasm. The Prudential 'Lifeline' effort, for example, includes Blood Donor Sessions – in the firm's time – First Aid training and volunteer street collections in aid of a local cancer care unit.

- The War Office Selection Board becomes the civilian Selection Board which becomes the Assessment which in turn becomes the Development Planning Workshop. The Pilkington Experience in motivating participants.

- The humanitarian dimension of motivation.

ACTION

- If your company is not already engaged in a worthwhile cause, ask today for suggestions and select a project by vote. Set up an all grades committee to discuss funding. Get the employees to organise the whole thing and 'own' the project, although you will take an active part and perhaps help with transport. Your aim should include better morale, breakdown of barriers, combating demotivating routine, useful Public Relations and team working. Your organisation will also be doing a considerable amount of good for the community which makes such projects a good example of MOTIVATION BY ENLIGHTENED SELF-INTEREST.

9. Personal Motivation

People whose job it is to motivate others must first be motivated themselves because the original driving force needed to get other people moving has to come from somewhere.

In fact we are all motivated by things, events and people outside ourselves, and our actions in response to these external motivating forces are governed by our conditioning and to a lesser extent by our inherited characteristics. In other words, the 'self-motivated' person most personnel managers are looking for is something of a myth.

TAKING CONTROL

Paradoxically, this is good news if you want to take charge of your own motivation because you can exercise a great deal of control.

For example, you can control many of the external stimuli by deliberately seeking M factors like inspiration, challenges and satisfactions. In this way you can control the quality and force of your own motivation.

You can also control your conditioning, changing it if necessary by training and ongoing education which can be as informal as a wide ranging reading programme or meeting new people. At the same time, while you cannot control your inherited characteristics, by recognising them you can allow for them and if need be limit their effects.

THE GOOD NEWS

This is good news if you suspect that you may not be as self-motivated as you would like to be, because it means that you have the power to change things.

In fact, this ability to control our motivation makes it look as though we are self-motivated, so we can continue to think in terms of John Adair's 50-50 rule, with 50 per cent of our motivation coming from outside and 50 per cent from within, and continue to use the convenient expression 'self-motivated', provided we realise that in the motivation stakes most of us start off, if not equal, then a great deal more equal than we have been led to believe.

PERSONAL MOTIVATION AND THE FIVE W'S

In all motivation situations the HOW? is governed by the WHO?, WHAT?, WHY?' WHERE? and WHEN? questions and this is especially true when you are motivating yourself.

These are the questions we must ask, and to answer them with anything less than complete honesty would defeat the purpose of the exercise. Such honesty is not easy to achieve as we are not always completely frank with ourselves.

WHO IS THE 'SELF' YOU NEED TO MOTIVATE?

We are all of us miraculous creatures, even though some of us may be fractionally more miraculous than others. Our bodies and minds are miraculous and, given the risks run by our ancestors and the hazardous mechanics of gene transmission, the fact that we are alive at all is a miracle in itself.

Reminding yourself that you are a 'miracle' can help give you a positive self-confident attitude towards personal motivation.

What has been done to this miracle and what you have done to it depend to a great extent on your 'culture', and your CV details will remind you about the person you wish to motivate, including your family background, birthplace, race, education, sporting achievements and social history. These in turn will tell you a lot about the attitudes and prejudices which control your reaction to M factors, including whether you regard them as +M or -M factors and, if so, to what degree.

Importantly, it will also remind you of your career achievements to date and your current position or status, an essential element in the WHO?

THE CHARACTER OF THE WHO?

With this information in mind you can then take a look at the inherited characteristics of the WHO? Are you, for instance, hard working or lazy and, if you are patently one or the other, how much of this was inherited and how much is the result of conditioning?

How intelligent are you? Innate intelligence is an inherited characteristic which is difficult to measure accurately, because people can be taught to score well in most intelligence tests. It is also easy to confuse intelligence with the effects of cultural advantages.

What are the dominant features of your personality? Are you ambitious or unambitious, cowardly or brave, selfish or unselfish, greedy or generous? These and other character traits are partly inherent but to a great extent are the result of lifelong conditioning – which means that if necessary they can be changed.

WHAT DO YOU WANT TO MOTIVATE YOURSELF TO DO?

Do you want to make more money, to gain a promotion, to win the approval of your superiors and colleagues or to get satisfaction from doing a better job? Remember that 'everybody wants something'.

You may decide that what you want to motivate yourself to become is a 'winner', but in that case you have to decide what you mean by winning. For example, winning is not all about money, although well motivated people will usually achieve a reasonable level of material success. The chief characteristic of genuine well motivated winners is that they are holistic winners and that they will have achieved this while helping other people to become winners, rather than by making them into losers.

WHY?

Asking why you are motivated to achieve a particular objective can sometimes put your aims in question. In extreme cases asking WHY? could prevent you from doing things you know to be wrong or unethical. Many people ruin their health and make themselves and others miserable in the attempt to achieve some particular goal without once asking themselves WHY? they want to achieve it. Others do ask themselves the question and do not like the answer.

For example, the high flying executives who quit the 'rat race' in the 1970s to go in search of the 'good life' were people who found themselves unable to answer the WHY? question.

While there is usually no need for such drastic measures, failure to answer the WHY? question satisfactorily almost certainly means that you need to change your career path or even your company.

WHEN?

You may cast a backward glance at the past as a standard of comparison and you should certainly think in terms of what your motivations are likely to be in the future, but the WHEN? you are most concerned with is NOW.

Your present age will almost certainly influence the way you react to different M factors, and affect the potency of value of factors like money, which often become of less immediate concern for the 'forty somethings'. Another important WHEN? is controlled by any deadlines you may have set yourself for the achievement of your main goals and intermediate ones.

WHERE?

WHERE? controls the environment in which you need to motivate yourself. Is it the right one for you? Is it motivating or the opposite? Should you change it? or move? WHERE? will also control the people who make up the workplace 'family' with whom many of us spend almost a third of our lives.

HOW DO I BECOME BETTER MOTIVATED?

One important way to increase personal motivation is to have a goal – and to write it down. The most effective way to do this is to write down a goal to be achieved by the end of next week, another by the end of next month, next year and so on, goals which should be reviewed regularly as a check on progress. Motivation specialists believe that only two per cent of managers do this and that they are among the most highly motivated and successful leaders.

You already know a lot more about what motivates or demotivates you than anyone else. Only you, for example, know of any secret fears you may have. Only you can quantify your motivations and establish an audit for your motivation in the workplace. In some ways this is like holding an Opinion Poll with only one respondent, and a prejudiced one at that, but it should enable you to establish the sort of personalised motivating package most likely to get you enthused about your job and compare it with the almost certainly generalised package on offer.

In this case the figure for NET motivation arrived at is an indication of your level of motivation and a means of getting you to think about personal motivation in an organised, positive way.

PREPARING A MOTIVATION AUDIT

Bearing in mind the answers to the W questions, here are some of the M factors you may consider important. Remember that each M factor should be expressed in such a way that it can be quantified as either plus or minus.

Assuming that your basic needs such as food, shelter and so on have been satisfied and will continue to be satisfied in the immediate future, these may still remain as – perhaps subconscious – fears and should therefore be classed under SECURITY.

MONEY – How important an M factor is money to you right now? Are you motivated by wanting more of it? In the context of the workplace, what would you be prepared to do to get it? Do you find it desirable for what it will buy or as a status symbol? Would another £10,000 a year motivate you ten times as strongly as an extra £1,000? What would happen if you lost your income?

PHYSICAL ENVIRONMENT OF THE WORKPLACE – How important is the look and feel of the place you work in? How much do you care about the decor, the equipment, the furnishings of your office, the state of rest rooms and public areas?

HEALTH – Are you motivated by the desire to achieve and maintain physical and mental health? Do you, for instance, consider your job to be stressful? (Are you worried – demotivated – by the possible effect of your job on your health?)

FAMILY – Are you motivated by the wish to give your family material things or is the quality of your family life more important? The answer to these questions could determine, for example, how much time you are prepared to devote to your job and whether you are prepared to move for a promotion. In any case, if you have a family, it is impossible to keep family and workplace apart, as even the act of trying to do so would have an M value. In many cases families are 'hostages to fortune'.

STATUS – How important a motivating factor is the status conferred by your job? Does the thought of retirement worry you, as you feel you will no longer be 'somebody'?

JOB SATISFACTION – Do you get a motivating charge out of the job itself or do you hate the thought of going to work every day to do the same routine job, in the same boring place, with the same boring people? If you get a great deal of satisfaction from your job you probably don't want to lose it. (See Security.)

CAREER PROSPECTS – Are you motivated by ambition? Is it

important to you to have a clearly defined career structure? – opportunities to change direction? – training and education opportunities, including regular assessments?

SOCIAL NEEDS – Decide on the M values you would allot to things like approbation, recognition, peer pressures. Are you clubbable or a loner? How much do you appreciate being praised by hierarchic superiors?

SECURITY – This is an M factor that could go off the scale. If you are an employee it gives your employer – no matter how you may both attempt to conceal it – a very powerful stick and an equally powerful carrot. Ironically, some of the ways in which he may seek to reassure you, i.e. more money and benefits, will increase its power. If you are a manager who is both employee and employer you should realise how powerful an M factor security can be.

SELF-ACTUALISATION – Self-actualisation is concerned with things like 'winning' in the holistic sense, fulfilling one's full potential, achieving autonomy, having a good feeling about oneself and having good relationships with other people. Self-actualised people are normally not too worried about security as they are confident of their ability to overcome temporary difficulties.

Everything motivates in some way so your list could go on for ever. Disregarding the insignificant factors, list any additional M factors that you consider important then do the sums.

How Does Your Workplace Compare?

You should now have a rough idea of your NET motivation and be in a position to establish how your notion of a personal motivation package compares with the motivation package currently on offer in your workplace.

If you are a completely autonomous entrepreneur the comparison will still be interesting, and closing the gap, if there is one, should be considerably easier than for any employee.

Preparing a Workplace Motivation Audit

Using the same list as the one used to calculate your own NET motivation you can now quantify the M factors in your particular workplace. Have they got the money right? How much are they using it as a motivating factor?

Do the sums to find out the NET motivation factor of the workplace motivation package?

How does the package compare with your personal package, i.e. the things that really motivate YOU?

The CAS Ratio

Almost all the senior managers we spoke to were able to quantify their CAS ratio – i.e. the ratio of 'carrot' to 'stick' motivation they were currently using to motivate their people – in a couple of seconds. You should now have a sufficiently clear picture of your personal workplace motivation to enable you to answer three important questions:

1. What CAS Ratio do you consider would be most effective in motivating you?

2. What is the CAS Ratio of your company's current motivation package, as on offer to you, and how does it compare with your idea of the perfect package?

3. Does the CAS Ratio of the motivating package on offer vary according to the status of the person or persons to be motivated?

WHAT CAN YOU DO TO INCREASE YOUR MOTIVATION

If you consider that you are not satisfactorily motivated by your company's motivation package there are several courses open to you:

(a) do nothing and hope for the best – unfulfilled hopes are exceedingly demotivating.

(b) change your company – a last resort but better than remaining unmotivated or wrongly motivated.

(c) change your role within the company – this can be a good move, but it is still drastic and the effects are not guaranteed.

(d) persuade the company to change its overall motivation package and, say, move in the direction of 'cafeteria' motivation in which employees help design their own package. Often a good move if you have enough clout or if there is the right sort of consultative machinery in place.

(e) examine your own attitudes (see audits) towards your company's motivation package for signs of prejudice, suspicion or apathy. Change your attitudes if need be. Change and broaden your 'culture' to lessen the effects of cultural conditioning, perhaps by taking full advantage of educational and training courses on offer. Change any demotivating minutiae of your job by, for example, cutting down on paperwork and increasing personal interaction. Ask WHY? For instance: why are you being asked to accept a heavier workload? There could be a good reason and maybe rewards in the pipeline but your immediate hierarchic superior may not be a great communicator.

Talk to people in your company who are highly motivated. In a perfect – or even half way reasonable – world the person you report to should be the one to motivate you, but this is not always the case.

For many reasons, not the least of which is that you 'own' the problem and are in control, (e) is often the way to go.

SUMMARY

- The self-motivated person. Personal motivation is largely a question of the force of external stimuli. The effects of such stimuli will be positive or negative according to your 'cultural' background, i.e. conditioning and inherited characteristics.
- Inherited characteristics are very important in determining how specific M factors motivate individuals and to what degree.
- Most of us have inherited characteristics which place us in the broad middle band. The things that could be preventing us from becoming fully motivated almost certainly include many which it is in our power to change.
- How to assess personal motivation and compare this with your company's motivation package.
- How to increase your motivation in the workplace by changing a) the package b) yourself.

ACTION

- If you are not already a 'list' person, begin making lists, especially in the workplace. Checking tasks off your list as you deal with them gives you a highly motivating, winning feeling which grows as the day, week or month goes on. If you are not already using one, invest in a good time management system.
- List your most important goals together with the dates by which you intend to achieve them. For instance, to have lost a given amount of weight by the end of next month or to have increased your income by a certain percentage. Flag these goals in your diary so that you are able to check your progress.

10. Motivating Individuals

Motivating other individuals, especially if the person concerned looks and talks much like us, seems as though it ought to be almost the same as motivating ourselves.

In fact, nothing could be further from the truth, and in most cases apparent similarities prove to be illusory, while obvious differences like sex, race and so on, are helpful signs that the person concerned may not share our conditioning or be motivated by exactly the same things in exactly the same way as we ourselves.

Women who seek to motivate men – or Japanese who seek to motivate occidentals – may well need to think twice about how they should do so, but at least the need for some special care is obvious.

By contrast, if you are seeking to motivate someone even as approximately similar to yourself as to share your sex and skin colour, especially if they also appear to share the same language, it is all too easy to assume that what motivates you will motivate them. This is rarely, if ever, the case.

In practice, a known shared background will help you to determine the motivation you use, but beware: not all middle class homes are the same, any more than are all upper class homes; not all schools of the same type provide exactly the same background and there is no way in which the individual you want to motivate can have shared exactly your workplace and social experiences. Even brothers and sisters are motivated differently, which is why, when motivating individuals, we must turn once again to the Five W's.

SOME QUESTIONS OF INDIVIDUALITY

First, the WHO? you are seeking to motivate has to be established and once again you will be attempting the equivalent of a Public Opinion Poll with only one respondent.

Because of this you should if possible have the individual's CV details in mind before you consider how to motivate them. You should also have any other information you can gather, including perhaps the views of intermediate supervisors. The need for individual motivation emphasises the need for managers to get to know the people who report to them. This sort of 'intelligence' will enable you to distinguish between, for example, an employee who would be motivated by a sideways move into a similar job, with the same status but different people, and a person who would be demotivated by changing his workplace 'family'.

WHAT? – Decide, and keep in mind, what it is that you want the individual to do.

Saying something like 'Fred. You're just going to have to shape up', for example, is not particularly motivating, while a specific instruction, preceded by consultation and followed by helpful suggestions, directs the motivating force in the way you intend the person to go.

WHY? – Always try to give your reasons for what you are asking an individual to do. The day of 'theirs not to reason why' is long gone; besides, they might come up with a better answer. For example, in the case of a sideways move, you should explain that you hope the move will help him or her to share new experience, inspire new enthusiasm and generate new ideas which will benefit everybody.

WHEN? – Pick a good time of day. You may be happy to work 18 hours a day and, when well motivated, your employees will not watch the clock, but in most cases five o'clock on a Friday evening is not prime motivating time.

The age of the individual or his length of service may be important factors. On the question of age gap in motivation, there is the example of the very senior railway official who helped a small

Geordie over a crowd barrier at Newcastle station so the lad could get a good view of Britain's wartime leader, only to be told scathingly, 'Mister Churchill? Howway man! A'm collectin' engine numbas!'

WHERE? – Privacy is best for individual motivation, with the exception of circumstances calling for praise and recognition.

Admonishing an individual in front of other employees may appear to get the message across but it is usually the wrong message.

A MOTIVATION AUDIT FOR THE INDIVIDUAL

You are now in a position to prepare a motivation audit in respect of the person you wish to motivate. You can do this in much the same way as your personal motivation audit and this will give you an idea of which buttons you should press in order to get the person concerned to do as you wish.

In practice, unless your need to motivate the individual to do exactly as you wish is vitally important, you will usually be able to work out their probable motivation audit in a matter of seconds. All you have to remember is that it will almost certainly not be the same as your own.

AN EMPLOYEE IS ALREADY AN 'INVOLVED' PERSON

Until comparatively recently the vast majority of the workforce – largely because of cultural conditioning – was not ready for a great deal of involvement.

The WHO? was different and the difference lay in the gulf between serfs, whose work was 'travail' – both the modern French word for work and the old English one are derived from the Latin for a three-pronged instrument of torture – and employees who were involved in the enterprise.

Most employees today are ready for involvement and when motivating individuals or groups this is one of the most powerful M forces available.

'ONE VOLUNTEER'

In the days of sail, shortage of manpower forced the Royal Navy to resort to the Press, a particularly violent form of conscription in which Press Gangs – motivated by bonuses – forced reluctant civilians to join the crews of their vessels, usually by clubbing them senseless.

The discovery that crew members recruited in this way were not always among the most effective resulted in the saying 'one volunteer is worth two pressed men'.

As a manager seeking to involve individuals in the achievement of company goals, you are attempting to engage them as volunteers, which will more than double their effectiveness. Some motivation experts believe that one volunteer is, in fact, worth as many as five pressed men.

This does not destroy the case for money motivation – once aboard, the pressed men of Nelson's time had much the same financial inducements as their fellows – but it does argue that INVOLVING TO SOLVE can make more than 50 per cent difference in effectiveness.

CHANGING 'WON'T' POWER TO WILL POWER

The involvement of a person's will rather than his or her reluctant compliance lies at the heart of modern motivation practice and a manager who can do this will have few motivation problems. However it is not always easy.

At the very worst a manager who asks someone to do something may find that they reply 'I won't', which usually means that they are not merely inert or unmotivated but are in fact negatively motivated or motivated in a direction other than that desired by the manager.

Changing this state of affairs can mean utilising many types of motivation but the manager should at least be able to rely on the individual listening to what he has to say.

THE AUTHORITY FACTOR

Potential KITA factors like the fact that you are paying their salary, or are responsible for doing so, will usually help you to gain and retain an employee's attention. Remember the reply of the Spanish peasant berated by an elderly English lady for flicking his donkey with a whip instead of speaking kindly to it. 'Senora, I will speak kindly to heem, once I have his attention.'

However, there is another important element in a manager's dealing with his subordinates and this is the currently fashionable factor of authority.

All employees, whatever their status, are already involved in their employer's activities from the moment they agree to take pay and have accepted – though perhaps with mental reservations – an often unspoken contract to obey the instructions of their hierarchic superior.

THE MOTIVATING POWER OF AUTHORITY

The M-value of authority should not be underestimated and not realising that one has power is almost as bad as abusing it. In 'Obedience to Authority' (Tavistock), S. Milgram describes an experiment in which 'ordinary decent men' were so seduced by the trappings of authority – in this case doctors' white coats and clip boards – that they did not refuse orders to go on administering what they erroneously believed to be electric shocks to a helpless 'victim' – in reality an actor – even when the control panel indicated that they had reached a point of the dial marked '450 volts – DANGER – severe shock'.

In fact, employees listen to their boss because they recognise that they have contracted to do so. It is up to managers to re-inforce this contract to the point where hierarchic authority is largely replaced by enthusiasm, sound leadership, encouragement, practical help, appeals to enlightened self-interest and the realisation that involvement is a two-way affair.

INVOLVING WITH A STAKE IN THE COMPANY

One effective way of involving employees is to give them a stake in the company but, as Robert Townsend points out in *'Further Up The Organisation'* (Coronet), not many people are involved in this way at the moment and 90 per cent of them have never even seen a stock certificate. What happens when people ARE involved is exemplified by the girl employee of the American Dana Corporation who said that ever since she got her first stock certificate she 'hadn't been throwing away pencils'. In much the same way petty theft went down dramatically once workers became stockholders, because they could see it was their money that was being stolen and were prepared to do something about it.

AN EMPLOYEE BUY-OUT

A prime example of motivation by financial involvement of this sort is the National Freight Corporation which until 1982, as British Road Services, was part of the National Freight Consortium which included Pickfords and Waste Management.

When Peter – now Sir Peter – Thompson, the company's first Chief Executive, organised what became known as the 'employee buy-out' half the 11,000 strong workforce and their families took part, with an average investment of £500, and bought the company from the government for £53.5 million. The stock market flotation in 1989 was very successful and today the company is valued at over £800 million. Immediate results of the 'employee buy-out' were a marked increase in employees' pride in their jobs, with an improvement in things like vehicle maintenance. All round performance went up and there was a feeling that the company had become a 'family.' Absenteeism went down to almost nil and peer pressure put an end to pilfering. Equally important is the fact that the Transport and General Workers Union who were wary of the scheme at first are now fully supportive.

New employees can get interest free loans to buy shares in the company for which there is an internal market and a BOGO or 'Buy One get One' plan.

Share applications are included in the 'Welcome to NFC' pack, which stresses that the Corporation is '. . . a team that spells success. Success for out customers, for our company and for us its employees and shareholders.' Everyone is totally committed to their customers because 'they not only work for NFC they own it.'

INVOLVEMENT NEED NOT BE FINANCIAL

Now the Group has 30,000 employees world wide, more than 90 per cent of whom own shares in the business, but although financial involvement, especially if workers are allowed to buy shares rather than are given them, is very effective, other methods of involvement work just as well. Part of the NFC success is due to the fact that employee shareholders do not have only a financial stake but, through shareholders' meetings – at which they have a double vote on all issues – and their own elected Shareholders' Director, have a say in how the business is run and who runs it.

IF YOU ARE REALLY INVOLVED IN WHAT YOU ARE DOING, YOU DON'T NEED TO OWN THE COMPANY – YOU ARE THE COMPANY.

MEN MOTIVATING WOMEN

Both men and women respond to involvement but in many ways women respond to a different, and possibly more idiosyncratic, motivation package than men.

We know one woman for instance who works for a hot-shot lawyer who sends her off to the other side of the globe at the drop of a contract. She admits to being motivated by his 'genius' and his eccentricity, which manifests itself in the form of encouraging handwritten notes and thoughtful gifts, like a loaf of his home-made bread or a book she has said she'd like to read.

Most women we talked to were anxious to tell us what things

they found demotivating about their male managers. These included 'talking down to me' – a frequent complaint – lack of respect, sexual innuendo, and being 'taken for granted', especially the assumption that in any group of equals if there was only one woman in the group it would always be she who was expected to make the coffee.

Other demotivating factors included: male managers moving target goalposts without warning; taking all the credit – in one case a male manager appropriated a case of wine sent by a customer as a gesture of appreciation to his female team – sexual harassment and blackmail. The demotivating aspects of poor leadership on individuals included male managers' lengthy non-business lunches and the cowardice of male middle managers in reporting upwards only the good news related to them by their female assistants. Women in middle management complained of the demotivating effects of male attitudes like 'She's doing a good job – for a woman'.

Of course there are some male managers who motivate the individual women on their staff brilliantly but it seems clear that if many managers were to reverse their present attitudes completely they would be doing a better job of motivation.

Women Motivating Men

Women now hold down top jobs – although not enough of them, apart from politicians, appear to get the very top jobs – and they seem to do best in the fields usually considered the toughest of all like journalism, PR and government service. This could mean that in these industries the men have begun to realise that 60 per cent of the national workforce and more than 50 per cent of customers are women.

Even at the very top, male attitudes can be disconcerting and not only in the West. When visiting the Far East some time ago we met a good looking, tough minded young woman who was at the very top of her particular Washington tree and was still seething about her demotivating encounter with Oriental businessmen. She told us that, while on a government goodwill mission to Tokyo, she had finished addressing a meeting of Japanese top managers on her specialist subject and was gratified by their applause, until their spokesman got up and said, 'That was interesting, but what does your boss think about it?' Her words as she explained to the individual in question that she was in fact the boss lost their motivating effect in translation.

Unfortunately, some women managers have chips on their shoulders which make them go on competing with their male subordinates even when they have won. The best women managers on the other hand know that all they have to do is to prove is that they can do the job well enough to earn respect and the men will fight for a sign of their approval.

WOMEN MOTIVATING WOMEN

A woman motivating another woman is like a man motivating another man – only more so. The good ones discover a motivating empathy which for example turns their secretary into a charming and super-efficient P.A.; the bad ones imitate the worst male bosses they have ever worked for and demotivate their juniors by talking down to them, taking them for granted and so on.

THE SECRET

It is difficult for both men and women managers to motivate individual subordinates of the opposite sex if the parents, siblings, teachers, friends, colleagues and partners of the manager in question have conspired to instil in them totally incorrect and demotivating attitudes.

However, good manners – an essential ingredient of sound managerial motivation anyway – is the real secret.

In this connection one way of ensuring that you get the motivation mix right is to 'promote' the person you wish to motivate.

For example, if the person in question is a colleague on the same grade as yourself, imagine that he or she is in fact your boss. You could be surprised by the careful way in which you arrange the time and place of the appointment to suit their convenience and prepare your case so as to take up as little of their valuable time as possible.

You could also find yourself rehearsing with care arguments which will, for example, suggest 'what's in it for them' will be more important to you than any benefits you might obtain for yourself.

Even the words you choose in which to put your motivating case will be subtly altered by this imaginary change in the WHO? In fact, your whole attitude may very well be different and you will stand a much better chance of achieving your objective.

Next time you want to motivate, say, one of your junior supervisors, you could try imagining that the person in question is a colleague of equal rank to yourself and here again you may well find that the care and consideration you show pay motivating dividends.

In the end of course – if you are not already doing so – you will find yourself treating everyone you wish to motivate with the same thoughtfulness and courtesy and will have learned one of the true secrets of motivation.

BEYOND INVOLVEMENT – EMPOWERMENT

It is not a lot of good – in fact it's counterproductive – to involve someone and get them really enthusiastic about their job while leaving them powerless to do anything about it. Don't get anyone fired up about tackling a problem unless you are prepared to let them 'own' it and to let them make mistakes, even if it is you who will 'carry the can'. You must also make sure that if money is involved they have control of sufficient funds to achieve the objective. In other words, as all detectives know, nobody will DO anything unless they have MOTIVE, MEANS AND OPPORTUNITY.

SUMMARY

- Motivating individuals. Different strokes for different folks means that there is a wider spectrum of important M factors – plus or minus – when dealing with individuals than with groups. By definition, effective motivation for individuals has to be individual and idiosyncratic.
- Don't make the mistake of believing that people who look like

you and share some of your background will share your motivations. If you have children you could already be aware of this.

- One volunteer is worth two pressed men – or women. Creating volunteers by motivating individuals can more than double the efficiency and productivity of your people – provided you also give them the means and the authority.
- The secret of successfully motivating people whose conditioning is different from your own, like people of a different sex, a different race, different background or different mental and physical capabilities, is 'good manners, good manners and, once again, good manners.'

ACTION

- Begin today asking yourself if the individual characters in plays or films you see, or books you read, really are sufficiently motivated to do whatever it is that the author requires them to do. Beware: analysing other people's motives is an essential management skill but it can become an obsession.
- Ask yourself if you have been consistently well mannered today, particularly to subordinates. If not, make a note to do some motivating fence mending.

11. Motivating Salespeople

Any company that fails to motivate its salespeople will soon go broke and one thing that makes salespeople special is that top management are reminded of this every time they look at the balance sheet. The other things that make them a special are the job they do and the sort of people they are, both of which have to be taken into account if you want to motivate them to bring in the business.

THE BUSINESS HUNTERS

More than any other employees managers have to deal with, salespeople resemble the hunters who roamed the earth before Man settled down to the business of agriculture and manufacturing.

More than any other employee, theirs are the motivations of the Pleasure Principle, including the excitement and challenge of the chase, the satisfaction of the 'kill' and the stimulating element of chance. Unlike most employees, the salesperson is immediately aware of his or her successes – and failures. For salespeople each day brings either joys or disappointments and they have very little time to be bored. Closely associated with, but very different from, the salesperson are the marketing people whose task is to seek out the best hunting grounds, prepare them where necessary and make sure that the salespeople arrive at them suitable armed. Like sales managers they are seldom brilliant salespeople.

WHO ARE YOUR SALESPEOPLE?

Today's salespeople are well trained professionals with a serious approach to their job but most of them – including many of the best – are role players who derive as much pleasure from a good performance as from seeing the customer's signature on the contract.

Often individualists rather than team players, they have a deep rooted and contradictory desire to be supported and encouraged. What they would really like is complete freedom, together with total company back-up, and reconciling the two factors is the problem of those who wish to motivate them.

If you are managing a salesforce you are fortunate if a proportion of the WHO? is in your control, because in no other department is it quite so essential to hire the best, train the rest and get rid of the pest.

WHAT DO YOU WANT YOUR SALESFORCE TO DO?

Of course you want your salespeople to sell, but it's not enough for a salesperson to persuade a customer to buy. If he makes enough calls, any clown with a decent line of patter will make sales; what he will not do is create customers.

The salesperson is your company's ambassador and it is on his attitude, his appearance, his performance and the quality of the service he provides, that your company will be judged by those whose opinion counts. Don't be misled by the monster ego of some salespeople – which often goes hand in hand with low self-esteem – or their sometimes violent personality swings.

Remember that what you are asking them to do is not always easy and that, while they will almost certainly be anxious to tell you about their triumphs and the difficulties they have overcome, they may not tell you about the rejections, the rebuffs and the occasional bits of sadism that are part and parcel of most salespeople's lot.

WHY DO YOU WANT YOUR SALESFORCE TO DO WHAT THEY DO?

You need salespeople to sell because their work ensures that the rest of the company can eat, buy cars and houses and send children to school. Salespeople are aware of this – but they need to be re-assured that you are aware of it too.

What they really need is to be certain that everyone in the company is aware of it.

WHEN?

Not all managers appreciate that for salespeople there is time – and there is selling time. Scheduling meetings, however potentially useful, during prime selling time is demotivating for your best salespeople. For those who are not so good it provides a ready-made excuse for poor figures.

Managers who deal with salespeople should be prepared to work long hours when in the field, with breakfast meetings and late night sessions. They should not call salespeople into Head Office without a very good reason.

WHERE?

Some sales territories are better hunting grounds than others and the temptation to give the best hunting grounds to the best hunters is great. This can lead to a situation where new, inexperienced and less than super salespeople face a 'Mission Impossible' every time they leave home, which can be very demotivating.

SO – HOW DO I MOTIVATE SALESPEOPLE?

Make sure you employ salespeople you can motivate; i.e. recruit the best. Then make certain that every one of them knows that the whole company recognises his, or her, contribution as a business getter and an ambassador.

Stress that you do not regard them as confidence men but as people worthy of confidence. (The word 'sell' is derived from the Latin 'consilium', meaning to advise or counsel and this is how they should see their role.)

It's Lonely Out There

Bearing in mind that you should eat into selling time as little as possible, set up an ongoing training programme designed to make salespeople familiar not only with the latest product knowledge but with production people and the rest of the troops. They are lonely; they need to be reassured that they are part of the company family. Even more important is to make sure that, when they need help in giving customers what they want, they should be able to pick up a phone in the customer's office and ask for the appropriate person in production or marketing – by name.

Make sure that any such phone calls are regarded as binding contracts and that no promises are made that cannot be kept. There are few things more motivating to a salesman than being able to demonstrate his ability to help the customer and nothing more demotivating than making promises he is unable to keep.

Show Your Appreciation

Salespeople need stroking. Telling them that they are great can be a self-fulfilling prophecy. In fact, like the American top salesman who was surprised that people should pay him for using his 'golden voice', most of them are people to whom words mean a great deal. If they are not doing well they are already getting enough put downs. What they need from you is appreciation of their efforts, encouragement, reassurance and practical help.

Give them the best available selling aids, ongoing training and a clearly defined promotion path for the potential leaders who may not always be the best salespeople.

Get the money package right. Make sure that your trainee salespeople have an adequate income – after all they are giving you their time and enthusiasm – and that all your salespeople have a basic income sufficient to live on and, where possible, slightly higher than the average income in your sector.

Once you have done this you are ready to start thinking about motivation incentives.

MOTIVATION INCENTIVES

Money

Like hunters, who like to be able to see and touch the results of their work, most salespeople enjoy the feeling that a portion of their earnings is visibly performance based, in the form of commission, preferably paid out immediately. They also enjoy bonuses and financial awards, but tend to regard money thus gained as stuff to be shovelled out of moving trains. The motivating effects do not last and non-winners tend to be demotivated.

Recognition awards

As hunters, salespeople enjoy trophies, applause and acclaim.

Merchandise

Trophies of the hunt that all the salesperson's family can enjoy. The salesman's home is where he is motivated to go hunting in the first place. It is where he returns to celebrate or to lick his wounds, after he has been to the pub to boast and tell tales of his marathon 'cringes' and desperate 'grovels'. The manager's job is to help make the salesman's home into a motivating comfort zone. Awards of even small luxuries can help motivate the middle 80 per cent of your salesforce, and help you to get more motivation for your money.

Travel

Travel awards are exciting and motivate both the salesperson and his or her family.

Money motivates salesmen up to a point but the rewards are those they cannot buy: a personal letter of commendation from the chairman or a chance to meet a sports celebrity, or a cruise – with a seat at the captain's table. The best motivation awards are those the recipient is still talking about ten years later.

A CAR IS NOT JUST A CAR

A salesperson's car is not just a car; it's a second home, an office, a retreat and comfort zone. When the world is treating them badly its trim is balm to the bruised ego, its smooth power a reassurance that there is at least one area of life that is under control; its badges and bolt-on goodies are status symbols which tell fellow knights of the road 'I'm doing well and my company appreciates me.'

Managers should spend some time in the field to discover for themselves the enormous M value of the car.

DON'T MOTIVATE SALESPEOPLE – MOTIVATE THE COMPANY

Don't motivate salesmen to the extent of neglecting the rest of the troops. For example, when Paul O'Hea took over as MD of Colt International, he discovered that 'being a very strong sales and marketing organisation, we had over the years over-emphasised our sales force to the detriment of those members of staff who worked in-house and were from time to time, regarded as second class citizens.' It's possible that you too could be devoting most of your motivation effort and budget to your sales division and leaving only the crumbs for other vital sectors. Don't worry – at least you are aware of the value of motivation. All you have to do now is to begin motivating everyone, but first take a look at why most managers motivate salespeople and see how many of the reasons apply just as much to the rest of the workforce.

WHY MANAGERS DO MOTIVATE SALESPEOPLE

1. The need is obvious

2. The return on investment of time and money is both immediate and quantifiable.
3. Salespeople meet customers and must be motivated to spread the company message.
4. Salespeople are out in the field and they need to be made to feel confident.
5. Salespeople are out of the office so you can't see that their heads are down as you can those of the people who share your building.
6. Salespeople are good company. You don't have to see them every day so if things are going reasonably well you can afford to relax.
7. Salespeople really appreciate your efforts. Give them an award and they'll come dashing up to collect it like a contestant on a TV game show.

WHY MANAGERS SHOULD MOTIVATE EVERYONE

1. The need is obvious – for one thing, if only the salespeople are highly motivated the rest of the troops will be demoralised.
2. The return on your investment of time and money will often be immediate and quantifiable. Many companies we selected as examples of best practice have found that motivating everyone who works for them is making millions of pounds difference.
3. Everyone in your organisation meets customers either external or internal and that makes motivating them important. Remember the impression of an organisation left by the last unmotivated person you spoke to on the phone or the last unhelpful or bad-mannered receptionist.
4. Everyone needs to be made to feel confident and to be reassured from time to time that what he or she does is important, especially if the job is unglamorous.
5. You may have forgotten your days in the ranks, but heads go down when the boss is on the prowl. It's during the rest of the time that people need motivation.
6. Your inside people are almost certainly good company if given the chance. You can motivate them and learn a lot at the same

time with a little judicious after-hours socialising. As for seeing them every day, you probably don't see those of salesman rank very often other than to nod to them.

7. Your job satisfaction starved staff will appreciate any motivation effort all the more for its novelty. You will be amazed how their appreciation translates into productivity, quality and cost effective initiatives.

... AND THERE'S A BONUS. Salespeople are often gregarious by nature but their job is almost always an individual one and the only times they get together are for training sessions and sales conferences.

By contrast, most shop-floor and office workers form natural groups, often depending on a common task. These are their workplace 'families', often becoming comfort zones which may even evolve their own language. We know of one office for example where a certain form is known as a 'blue Clive' or simply a 'Clive' after the chap who once handed them out.

These natural teams are of great importance for managers introducing quality circles and the like, because in addition to being the second building block of your organisation they give rise to the phenomenon known as synergy.

SYNERGY – THE ENERGY OF THE TEAM

Synergy is the working together of two or more forces – in our case those of people – to produce an effect greater than the sum of their individual effects. It is noticeable for example in sports teams but is present in all teams, especially the natural teams of the workplace. Synergy – the word comes from the Greek and means 'working together' – has a very high M value, which need not necessarily be positive, and is a key factor in motivation.

It is the business of managers to see that teams are motivated in such a way as to produce the maximum synergy and to ensure that the power generated by the team is directed in a positive way rather than dissipated like steam from a kettle. The best way to accomplish this is to make sure that each team has a challenging but achievable goal, together with a well defined remit, and that a structure of leader/coaches ensures two-way communication with management.

Preparing a Motivation Audit

Once you have decided that it is necessary to motivate not only your sales staff but every member of your company the next step is to prepare a motivation audit for your organisation.

The questions should be expressed in such a way as to enable you to give each element a value ranging from one to ten.

Once you have prepared your audit, do the sums to find your organisation's current motivation status.

Here is a suggested audit. You can add any other factors you consider important, always provided you use the same list when you prepare a fresh audit to demonstrate your motivating success in, say, three months' time.

Twenty Questions

1. Basic pay and benefits package?
2. General environment; approach, reception, public rooms?
3. Appropriate and stimulating working environment; decor and furnishings of workshops and offices?
4. Equipment; up to date and in good working order?
5. Management; good leadership?
6. MBWA or management by walking about?
7. Adequate customer visits, external?
8. Adequate customer visits, internal?
9. Induction programme for new employees?
10. Training programmes and internal promotion opportunities?
11. Sickness and work re-organisation procedures?
12. Health and fitness; appearance of staff?
13. Informal after hours mixing between managers and staff? Are there sporting events organised by staff?
14. Possibilities for sideways moves – job swapping?

15. People appointed and briefed where appropriate to take charge in case of unexpected events like fires, medical emergencies?
16. Punctuality of people arriving for work, starting and finishing meetings etc.?
17. Attendance? i.e. much absenteeism?
18. Time management? i.e. much time wasting?
19. Honesty: i.e. is there petty theft – abuse of personal phone calls?
20. General state of the organisation's morale?

You now have an idea of your company's personality profile and how it may look to the people who work for it. If the overall picture is depressing there are a number of factors over which you have partial or total control; others which you can control only indirectly or perhaps merely influence.

You may feel that it would be helpful to call in professional motivation consultants who will almost certainly have already met and overcome the sort of motivation problems you have.

SUMMARY

- Motivating salespeople – the individuals who are more individualistic than most.
- The special needs of salespeople. The importance of the motor car as a motivator.
- Why you shouldn't motivate salespeople at the expense of the rest of your organisation.
- Establishing a motivation audit for the company using real numbers.

ACTION

- Establish a motivation audit for your company. Send out the 'Twenty Questions' to as many of your employees as possible and ask them to give their rating – anonymously – on the motivational standards of their workplace.

12. The Role of the Motivation Specialists

The business of the motivation consultant is the motivation of business – your business.

Once you have decided to motivate the whole of your organisation, or to experiment with a single division as a control, the consultant can help you make a motivation audit, diagnose possible weak spots and suggest appropriate remedies.

He will help you get started, usually with a targeted and structured motivation campaign, and show you the way forward.

He will also make sure you are aware that it is you and your staff who will be the motor of the ongoing motivation effort. He is there to fuel the first motivation, to switch on the engine, demonstrate its power, show you how to steer the effort in the way you wish it to go and oil the wheels if necessary.

After that, apart from his checking to make sure all is well, you will be very much on your own – you, and your newly motivated, success oriented team, that is.

CHOOSING A MOTIVATION SPECIALIST

You can find a motivation specialist in the Yellow Pages or have one recommended by an enthusiastic and satisfied client. Either way you should make sure that the agency you choose is staffed by dedicated and experienced professionals, with a successful track record you can check with a couple of phone calls.

You will probably be invited, along with the appropriate members of your staff, to attend a motivation seminar – perhaps preceded by a motivating champagne breakfast – where senior members of the consultancy will tell you how they go about motivating businesses like yours.

MOTIVATING FACTORS

At the seminar you will hear a great deal about factors we have already discussed like: involvement, recognition, empowerment, achievement, challenge, adventure, status, helping others, fear, pride, teamwork and the big four: LEADERSHIP, PLANNING, DEADLINES and WINNING.

You will also hear about the consultancy's campaigns – perhaps an ideas Campaign like IML Employee Involvement's 'Make a Difference' (MAD).

In the past, management has not always taken employee involvement in generating new ideas seriously enough. This is because:

1. they thought they had plenty of ideas of their own and were already desperately trying to action the ideas of their boss.
2. they knew they would have to reject most of the ideas and didn't know how to go about it.
3. they feared they would be embarrassed by good new ideas that would show them up in a poor light.
4. they had asked for ideas in the past and received very few.
5. traditional suggestion schemes even with the promise of substantial financial awards had proved ineffective.

Meanwhile the employees were reluctant to make suggestions because they feared being regarded as a 'teacher's pet', thought the manager was too busy and wouldn't listen anyway, and were afraid of being laughed at if their idea was thought to be stupid.

THE JAPANESE DISCOVER COUEISM AND CALL IT KAIZEN

Modern management appreciate that the WHO? has changed and that their better educated, better informed and more caring staff are prepared to accept involvement in improving performance, quality and therefore profit, which is at long last achieving respectability.

Japanese companies like Toyota have shown that not only can individuals practise the principles of Emile Coué, who asserted 'Every day in every way I am becoming a little better', but that *Kaizen* or 'continuous improvement involving everyone' is possible.

Motivation campaigns demonstrate how to achieve *Kaizen* in practice and an in-house report on a 'Make a Difference' Campaign run by the Benefits Agency, an Executive Agency of the Department of Health and Social Security, illustrates how this happens.

THE BENEFITS AGENCY EXPERIENCE

When the DSS created the Next Step Executive Agencies Michael Bichard became the Chief Executive of the largest of these, the Benefits Agency. He was faced with the problem of changing the culture of an enormous Government Department seen as old fashioned and whose staff were not perceived as necessarily thinking of the people claiming benefit as 'customers'. He used the IMLMake a Difference (MAD) involvement campaign in many parts of the country to provide the original impetus for the change as part of a long term strategy.

One of the first test campaigns, which was run in the Preston District Office from 27 April–22 May 1992, worked on an average staff-in-post figure of 222. Those responsible later reported as follows.

The first steps were the appointment of a Chief Co-ordinator who was responsible for the effective running of the campaign, and two Vice Co-ordinators who were responsible for the day to day running of the campaign, including the selection and support of team leaders, the distribution of campaign materials and the logging and monitoring of all ideas. Also appointed were four Assessors to investigate, assess and implement Category 2 ideas in liaison with the Chief Co-ordinator, and twenty-five Team Leaders charged with briefing all team members and encouraging their participation, plus a MAD News 'Editor' responsible for the publication of a weekly newsletter.

SETTING A TIMETABLE

The report goes on to detail the timetable of the campaign which was preceded by a briefing of MAD leaders by the Chief Co-ordinator and the display of campaign materials.

The campaign proper began with a Teaser Week designed to get people's attention, followed by a first ideas Generation Phase lasting 12 days and designed to look at small ways in which staff could make improvements which would 'Make a Difference' to their job. This was followed by a second ideas Generation Phase in which people identified their main customers – primarily internal customers, and looked at ways of 'Making a Difference'.

THE CAMPAIGN IN PROGRESS

The agency's report continues: 'On entering the building on the morning of 27 April staff were confronted by 4ft cardboard dinosaurs and posters displaying the initials MAD. First reaction was mixed but the aims of getting people's attention and rousing them from their apathy were achieved. Once the staff were made aware that prizes would be awarded for their humorous interpretations of the MAD initials, ideas came flooding in, some of which were even repeatable.

'On Thursday 30 April the ideas campaign was launched – the real definition of MAD was explained. As an incentive to staff to participate a mug, resplendent with the office logo, was presented to each member of staff on receipt of their first idea.

'These were categorised as Category One ideas which were actioned by the MAD originator/leader with the agreement of his or her line manager and implemented without delay, or Category Two ideas which went beyond the jurisdiction of MAD leaders and were passed by the Co-ordinator to the Chief Co-ordinator and then to the relevant assessor for handling.

'Each idea submitted gained automatic entry into the Prize Draw, whether the idea was implemented or not, i.e. the more ideas submitted the greater the chance of winning.

'A high percentage of Category One ideas were implemented during the campaign and rivalry for rosettes awarded for these provided an element of fun.'

The report stressed that it would take many weeks before all the Category Two ideas had been assessed but that the people submitting these ideas had been told who was responsible for looking into the idea and for reporting back to them in the long term.

MAD AND THE CUSTOMER

The second phase 'brought new life into the campaign midway through the third week'. Sixty-nine customer ideas were put forward on the first day, all of which qualified for the award of a MAD pen.

CONCLUSIONS ON A CAMPAIGN

The report concluded that the campaign had been 'without doubt a success'. Participation was due to inspiration of team leaders and time spent was not lost, since involvement led to 'a higher rather than a lower output of work.

'The campaign was "challenging", but this improved teamwork throughout the office. THE REALISATION THAT WE HAVE INTERNAL CUSTOMERS WAS A REAL BREAKTHROUGH AND HELPED TURN "THEM AND "US" INTO "WE".'

The campaign encompassed all four core values: the staff came up with real ideas to improve Customer Service. It demonstrated that the Manager and his Management Team are receptive to ideas and initiatives from their staff. There was a bias for action in so far as ideas were being assessed with regard to the possibility of both short and long-term changes. Ideas gathered by the campaign led to better working conditions for staff and an increase in staff efficiency, showing 'value for money' benefits.

Of the 204 employees eligible to take part, 185 people submitted a total of 641 ideas, 308 of which were Category One ideas of which 205 have been implemented.

The assessors also received 333 Category Two ideas.

The results of this kind of involvement are impressive but involvement also lends itself to a more structured campaign.

STRUCTURING MOTIVATION

Alastair Black, IML Employee Involvement's Operations Manager, says of the company's FIT programme:

'Since 1976 we have been concerned with employee involvement in the field of "ideas" campaigns, which the FIT programme takes one step further.

'An ideas campaign is voluntary and enables people to put forward their ideas on improving the organisation at all levels.

'What the FIT programme does by means of a structured project is to provide everybody throughout the organisation with a series of quality improvement activities, which are then monitored by management in order that improvements can be put in place.'

THE FIVE PRINCIPLES

Alastair Black goes on to explain the Five Principles:

1. The FIT programme is an in-house programme designed to reflect the structure of your organisation, making sure that the benefits are long-term.
2. The programme requires the whole-hearted participation of everyone. Management need to be obsessed about quality if you are going to get enthusiasm to filter down to involvement at all levels.

3. We are asking people to come forward with positive ideas. We are not offering people direct financial rewards. The real reward of the FIT programme comes when people realise that they can improve the quality of life in the workplace.
4. The programme is based on a sporting analogy designed to be enjoyable and fun.
5. The programme is structured, controllable and has a series of built-in deadlines.

THE SPORTING ANALOGY

The FIT Programme – no doubt spurred on by the fact that Alastair's brother Roger is a member of Britain's 4×400 metres Olympic Relay Team – uses the analogy of the track relay team, stressing the fact that some teams of brilliant individuals don't win on the day because they lack the awareness of the other people around them.

The aim, says Alastair, is to improve the quality of service between internal customers and suppliers and to cut down the profit lost by inferior quality, i.e. by failing to get things right first time – rated by Sir John Harvey Jones at 20 per cent in manufacturing industries and 40 per cent for service industries. 'There is a significant cost of quality internally which we can do something about by learning how to pass the baton without dropping it.'

SETTING UP A MOTIVATION PROGRAMME

The person responsible for the programme happening is the Senior Manager on site. Then comes the Programme Organiser, the liaison between management and consultant and the focal point of the programme's organisation.

Before the programme starts the whole organisation is split up into a number of natural working groups.

'Each team has a leader responsible for making sure its activities are productive. These are the Team Captains, but we also need Coaches, which is where the management people come in to look after the psychological element and lay down the standards before you begin. They are accountable collectively to the Head Coach or Senior Manager, who lays down minimum training or coaching standards which are fed down through the organisation by individual coaches who set the standards for each of their individual teams.'

The Sports Theme

Alastair explains that the rest of the FIT programme follows the sporting analogy, with 'workouts' in the 'gym', preceded by 'warm ups', taking the place of meetings.

Phase One

Phase One is the 'warm up' phase of the programme during which for two or three days people are asked, for example, to guess what FIT stands for.

Warm ups and workouts take place in 'Gyms' isolated from the workplace. They have all the necessary equipment in the way of furniture, stationery, blackboards and so on but there are no telephones or fax machines.

Phase Two

Phase Two begins with a company-wide presentation explaining the programme, in the course of which everyone receives a course manual. It continues with team 'workouts' in the gym, during the first of which each team identifies the three other teams they see as being their main customers.

Phase Three

They then ask each customer team to suggest three areas in which they as a supplier team could make improvements. The programme, Alastair stresses, is 'customer led and project driven', so the supplier teams ask what the customer wants. In the case of a company with around 400 employees this phase lasts three to four weeks, at the end of which every team in the organisation will end up with nine improvement projects.

PHASE FOUR

During Phase Four, which lasts three to four months, teams begin – by means of workouts – to implement their nine improvement projects. By this time the teams are motivated, so that once the original nine projects have been put in hand they begin to look for other possibilities of improvement and request more and more workouts in what soon becomes a natural and ongoing process,

Throughout the programme coaches use a ten-point appraisal system to evaluate the performance of individual teams, an evaluation they have to justify to their fellow coaches – and the Head Coach.

THE COLT EXPERIENCE

Paul O'Hea is the Managing Director of Colt International Ltd, a sister company of the Colt Group, a £100 million business started by his grandfather in 1931. He studied accountancy, engineering and languages before working in Europe, and later held a job with a Colt subsidiary in London before his first senior appointment as Marketing Manager for Colt International. When he took over as MD he felt that the group's strong sales force was being motiviated to the detriment of the other members of the staff.

'There was another motivation problem because there was a feeling in the business that we were overmanned. I knew I would have to do some cutting and the staff knew this before I did. Over the years we had added to the departments and we had become cumbersome and that in itself created a motivation problem because nobody had a real job.

'I hadn't been trained in motivation theory, I'd picked up my ideas by osmosis from a father and an uncle who have been in the business for forty years.

'I had a foundation on which to build in the importance we place on the individual, the ethics of the family business and our belief that "everything we do should be of benefit to Mankind". This is fine but it is useless if you can't put it into practice.'

Moving into Motivation

'The typical company briefing that had gone on over the years had been at such a level that nobody could understand anything – so much so that when we brought it to the people it was terribly demotivating. Nobody wanted to ask questions in case they made fools of themselves. Nobody was responsible for motivation which tended to be left to the Board of Directors.

'Quality was already on the agenda – we've gone through that barrier. Now we are beginning to mention motivation at board meetings.'

Talking to Unions

Talking to the Unions paved the way for Colt's motivation effort. Said Paul, 'I introduced meetings with the union representatives. I've had two hour-and-a-half meetings so far and I'm going to hold one a month now, if not more. They have probably changed the face of Colt.

'The unions were constantly having to battle with middle management. OK, they got a bit aggressive back in the 1970s, but when you talk to these people they don't want to ruin companies. They are desperate to move forward. They were getting awful information from middle management – all wrong and distorted.'

Launching a Total Quality Management Programme

'We have 400 people in the UK and now we've launched a TQM programme because we found there were too many people in different departments who didn't know what they were doing.

'The quality of the work was desperately bad, so how on earth could we satisfy our external customers? We discovered it was more important to get the internal motivation right and that the improvement in internal quality would transfer itself to the customer.

'We used relay runner Roger Black for the launch, after which we broke Colt down into teams who identify customers and ask what really upsets them and how can they put it right.

'For instance, I have a team and we identified the Personnel Department as "customers" and when we asked them what we could do to better the service it all came out. There was motivation due to the fact that we could communicate.'

'It's Working – That's the Main Thing'

'The idea is that there is no hierarchy in this programme at all. Every member of Colt is involved and has the opportunity to change it. Even I have no control over what the various teams come up with.'

Of course, the 'control', not of ideas but of their assessment and implementation, is part of the structured motivation campaign.

Paul says: 'The fact that we got someone in from outside indicated that it wasn't just management fiddling around.

'We had our first award session recently when I gave out bronze, silver and gold medals. Okay, they're just a bit of metal on a ribbon but the fact that we recognised there was a winner was appreciated.

'It's working – that's the main thing. I hope it will go on doing so ad infinitum.'

Motivating Changes

Before they began their campaign Colt had neglected their buildings but are now renovating the kitchen and have invested in new furniture and 'superficial refurbishments' – painting and lighting.

Other changes include coat badges like Paul's which reads 'Head Coach'. More importantly, continuing the motivating 'involve to solve' theme, the Company now 'cascades' its briefing sessions.

Said Paul, 'We now finish our board meetings an hour earlier than before and then brief the senior managers, who then go away and brief everyone else down to the most junior on the shop floor.

'So far our motivation efforts have taught the managers about what makes people tick and made them aware that people on the shop floor are intelligent and have very good ideas. Some people who haven't uttered a word in years are now talking.

'I believe that by giving people the opportunity to make their jobs easier they actually make them better, so they get more out of them, they stop being frustrated and have less remedial work to do, so they are not spending half their lives backtracking.'

The Bottom Line

'We are using no financial inducements whatsoever. The amount of work that has to be redone is going down and our objective is to save a million pounds in the first year.'

Summary

- The business of motivation consultants is to motivate your business. Go for one with a track record.
- Involve to Solve. Why managers were reluctant to involve employees and how motivation consultants are changing their minds by introducing *Kaizen*.
- An Ideas Campaign. The Benefits Agency Experience – a successful mix of fun, ideas and new motivation.
- Taking the Ideas Campaign a step further. Introducing a structured Campaign. The Colt Experience. On course to save £1 million in first year. MD says, 'The main thing is – it works'.

Action

- Check the loss of profits in your company due to lack of quality. If it is anything like the 20 per cent–40 per cent Harvey Jones says is the norm, your motivation audit has almost certainly identified a motivation problem.
- Check the list of reasons management has been reluctant to take involvement seriously. Do they remind you of your management team? If so, you might be able to use some targeted advice on getting your staff motivated.

13. Motivating a Miracle – The Unipart Experience

Imagine a company where the hourly paid workforce worked for four hours, slept for four hours and then got overtime to clear up the backlog – all with the tacit agreement of the management.

It sounds incredible but the nightmare company really existed and, as the Service and Parts Division of British Leyland, was part of a once great giant that had become a joke.

That was in 1974 and what is even more incredible is that the same company, now known as the Unipart Group of Companies, is currently one of the leading automotive parts companies in Europe – on course to becoming a world class winner with sales of around £600 million a year of which 20 per cent are export.

Perhaps more remarkable still is a story in the Group's latest Annual Report about a young part-time cleaner who stepped into the breach when illness struck the staff of her branch, made sales, answered queries, manned the phone and 'enabled the branch to keep faith with its customers'.

Evidently, the staff of Unipart are no longer prime customers for the mattress business.

A PROBLEM OF INERTIA

The Rip van Winkle workers – who, to the great joy of the press, really did smuggle mattresses into their workplace – were symptomatic of a company that had lost its motivation and was inert in the strict meaning of the word.

Not for them the pleasures and challenges that motivated the hunter gatherers, not for them the compulsions that drove men to the trenches, or indeed any but the lowest in the Hierarchy of Needs. They had no hint of the 'noble cause' Major General Scott Grant considers one of the greatest motivations of all, nor of the excitement that Blashford-Snell shows people how to generate by forming action teams to serve others. Worse still, they had none of the all-ranks leadership which is a truly British heritage, because many of their managers, faced with a classic 'Theory X' workforce, had abdicated their responsibilities.

Not that the sleeping workers were unintelligent; after all they were clever enough to beat the system, increase their income and provide themselves with enough union clout to protect them from the consequences.

However they were a different WHO? from the staff of today, prisoners of their culture and the direct heirs of the 'hands' who manned the dark satanic mills of the Industrial Revolution, with an ingrained 'them' and 'us' adversarial attitude resulting from more than two centuries of mainly 'stick' motivation.

Like the demoralised army that General Montgomery took over on the eve of Alamein they were in desperate need of inspiration and a leader who would generate positive NET motivation in the desired direction.

ENTER THE CHARISMATIC LEADER

John Neill, the Group Chief Executive of UGC – the Unipart Group of Companies – who joined the company in 1974 when it was still a Division of Leyland, remembers the sleeping workers well and says of the motivation and morale of the workforce in those days: 'I'm lost for words, it was so bad. They were on a collision course with management, with the company and with the customer.'

In fact, as was the case in many companies, a highly motivated and enthusiastic Sales and Marketing division was happily fuelling the Titanic while others, in John's words, were 'doing everything in their power to outwit and screw the company.'

Fortunately in January 1987 a management buy-out gave John the opportunity to put things right and the group discovered that it was led by a man with a mission to motivate.

John Neill, who has always wanted to be a businessman, has a BA and a Masters degree in business administration from Strathclyde University, where he studied the work of the motivation gurus and managed a number of student organisations including the Students Union and the Conservative Club. He was also President of AISEC – an association for the international exchange of students within commerce – a 'formative experience' as he had to motivate his peers to work for the Association at the expense of their degrees.

He also learned the importance of a sound, enduring philosophy, commitment, energy and enthusiasm.

The Mission Statement

John believes that one of the problems of the West has been the search for instant solutions. 'Unipart's success is due to the fact that we have had a coherent and consistent set of values in our management for a very long time. The philosophy which we articulated in 1987 has endured to this day and that is to understand the real and perceived needs of our customers better than anyone else, and to serve them better than anyone else.'

By the late 1980s Unipart had formulated its group mission and the mission statement which, John believes, is a fundamental part of the group's corporate planning process.

The mission statement begins: 'The Unipart Group of Companies aims to be an enduring upper quartile performing company in which stakeholders are keen to participate . . .'

THE 'WHO?' BECOMES A STAKEHOLDER

The word STAKEHOLDER is important to Unipart and includes their employees, their customers, their suppliers, the communities in which they operate and their investors.

The mission will be accomplished, says the statement, by 'pursuing our values, pursuing well judged entrepreneurial risks, ensuring the continuing relevance and synergy of the divisions' missions and creating an environment within which the divisions can and do pursue their mission.'

At the theatrical Epcot show held in 1987 to launch the privatisation of the group John Neill announced that the corporate goal would be 'to make the UGC logo a mark of outstanding personal customer service'.

How he set about accomplishing the corporate goal is a classic example of motivation in practice.

ABOLISHING 'STICK' MOTIVATION – OR NEARLY

Unipart's CAS Ratio has been heavily 'carrot' oriented from the beginning. John Neill himself believed that they had virtually abolished the 'stick' factor and was one of the few managers to have difficulty in establishing a CAS Ratio for his organisation. In fact, people are often understandably apprehensive about losing even the best of jobs with the best of companies and remain concerned about possible censure by superiors and workmates, so the 'stick' never disappears completely. Even so, the Unipart CAS Ratio must be around 90-10, which has to be something of a record.

Close to the beginning of their motivation effort Unipart ran a Putting People First Programme – a project from Time Management International – with the aim of 'helping each and every one of us to look after our customers so well they prefer to deal with us rather than any other supplier.'

As John put it in a foreword to the Putting People First, 'You

Make the Difference Course' – the Unipart 'U' was a piece of serendipity – 'There's nothing to stop us turning this company into not just a place to be proud of but the best place we've ever dreamed of working. What if we each played our part in building the company of our dreams? Why not! If we can dream it we can do it – and have a lot of fun in the process.' It was a clear statement of a return to the Pleasure Principle.

You Make a Difference

The course itself was designed to help people achieve a balance between their private lives and the workplace, to define their goals, to learn how to use their 'unlimited' brain power, to remove some of the causes of stress, to improve communication, to take control, to think positively and to be winners rather than losers. It was designed to be 'a major catalyst' in the creation of a culture 'in which everyone is committed to personal development, improved teamwork and outstanding customer service.'

At the same time the company introduced a share ownership scheme which would enable all employees to participate in the growth of the enterprise. Said John, 'We keep explaining to people how risky and difficult our industry is but, if we are successful, in the course of a 20 year working lifetime any individual ought to be able to generate capital beyond his normal expectations, had he been an ordinary employee on salary.'

At the time of the buy out, more than half of the Unipart employees chose to become shareholders, 'which was double the number predicted by City experts' and the long term shareholding of management and employees is now 47 per cent, which means that the company is really controlled by its management and employees. 'I believe it's an extremely important factor in achieving commitment to the company, to the customer, to quality and to continued improvement.'

Participation and its Implications

In 1990, for the first time, Unipart paid a dividend which at 10p was the equivalent of twice the original 1987 acquisition cost of ordinary shares. 'In 1992 for the year ending December 1991 we doubled the dividend – to 20p – when most companies were either cutting dividends or struggling desperately to hold on', said John. 'It has had a very motivating effect on all our stakeholders. We wholeheartedly support the principles of wider share ownership and particularly employee share ownership. It's quite tough to make it happen; it's a difficult, long-term exercise but I think any company can do it, and should do it. It's what management is all about – making companies work.'

Unipart views all its employees as 'key stakeholders' but continues to take pride in the fact that so many of them are also shareholders. The latest move in this direction has been a new share buying opportunity which made share options available to employees on the basis of their personal performance. More than £1 million worth of shares was required to meet the response from employees.

A Focus on New Ideas

As a company, John Neill stressed, Unipart prefer to develop things in-house but are happy to learn from other people and in the early days, for example, hired a clinical psychologist to 'plumb the deep seated needs' of their customers, so that they could design what the customer really wanted.

'We don't suffer from NIH – Not Invented Here – but we do have a lot of experience of motivating and communicating. However we wanted to do something immediately after the privatisation which would give everybody a chance to focus on dreaming up new ideas and putting them into practice and QED was a ready made package.'

QED, like 'Make a Difference', is an IML ideas campaign designed to get people to contribute to cost and quality management by harnessing their potential enthusiasm for improvement. After a 'Teaser Week' during which everyone is asked to suggest what QED stands for, people are asked to look at their own job areas and submit ideas for small improvements that will save a 'Quid Each Day'. Later in the campaign the emphasis changes to 'Quality Each Day', but the savings – most of which are recurring – are only one benefit of the project which aims to change attitudes and improve morale.

As John Neill put it, 'It provided a surge of motivation on the back of what was a terrifically successful organisation; it provided a focus for people to get involved and have a go – and it was fun.'

PUTTING PEOPLE FIRST

Unipart's next major motivation move was to run the PPF programme. 'We were impressed by what British Airways had achieved. I believe they are the best airline in the world to fly with and that's a contrast because they used to be the worst.

'We saw many of the ingredients of PPF as being highly relevant to our business but we did spend time with the PPF team and made some changes to the programme. In fact we wrote the music to remind people of the key messages in the style of songs from the Epcot Show like "I am my Company" and "Positive Strokes."

'What PPF does over a period of two days is to create an environment in which a cross section of employees from top to bottom can sit together and experience together with, say, the Managing Director of Edmunds Walker sitting next to a sales rep from Unipart International and a manufacturing guy from Unipart Industries. It focuses on a whole lot of personal as well as company issues, and illustrates in a very powerful way the importance of interpersonal behaviour and how an individual with a negative attitude can really depress and demoralise all those around him compared with the motivating effect of someone who has a positive attitude.'

Motivating Personal Service

'One of the most powerful examples is the way they differentiate between material and personal service. For instance, if you go into a restaurant and get very good quality food, that is very good material service, but if the waiter drops the food in your lap and is uncaring and rude you probably won't go back to the restaurant, no matter how good the quality of the food or how much trouble the manager has gone to.

'By contrast, if the food is not very good that day, but you get marvellously attentive personal service, and the manager apologises and explains what has happened and invites you back, you probably will go back.

'If you combine outstanding material service with outstanding personal service then you have that customer for life.'

Unipart have invested heavily in material service including, for example, spending £750,000 on roll cages to speed up stock orders. They now realise that the importance of personal service includes personal service to the internal customer. Said John Neill, 'Our company has a history of being customer focused and we wanted this customer focus to permeate everywhere, not just the sales and marketing group. It was this that led to the Mark in Action programme.'

A Home Grown Recognition Programme

The Mark in Action Programme, which began in 1989, was a logical step in Unipart's motivation evolution and was based on research into recognition programmes run by companies throughout the world, combined with an understanding of the company's own heritage.

Under the programme, any individual or team providing outstanding personal customer service 'beyond the normal call of duty' can be nominated for a Mark in Action award.

The company appointed as manager of the programme a young

woman executive with considerable missionary zeal who has ownership of the programme and has made it come alive.

Any team or individual can be nominated by their peers, by their manager or by their customer, and the nominations are checked with line managers or by the manager of the programme before being submitted to two independent judges who decide whether to make the award or not. Revealingly, not everyone gets an award, and they are becoming harder to get because 'what was outstanding two or three years ago is now normal.'

Those who don't get an award receive a letter from the Programme Manager thanking them for what they have done. Those who do are invited to the monthly ceremony at which the awards are presented by the Chief Executive, in front of the entire line management above the individual or team that earned the award. The fact that the winners are always outnumbered by directors is an indication of how seriously the company takes the programme.

Award winners get an 18ct gold pin, their names are inscribed in a book held in Reception at Unipart House, their photographs are distributed throughout the company and their stories are told on *Grapevine* – the company's regular video.

A TOUCH OF RESPECT

There are no financial rewards for Mark in Action winners who, in addition to their pin, get a small gift, usually something for their partners, and an invitation to a lunch party with their managers, but they do now get a Unipart share as a 'token of respect',

Not surprisingly, many people who have won Mark in Action awards have gone on to do extremely well in the company.

MOTIVATING TO BECOME WORLD CLASS

In 1991 Unipart began a World Class Crusade, the aim of which was to see the company ranked alongside the organisations whose logos have become universally recognised symbols of World Class.

With this in mind, a 'My Contribution Counts' programme was

launched with a course, prepared in house, which linked a psychological approach to the day to day life of the company to focus on the possibilities for all-round individual improvement.

OUR CONTRIBUTION COUNTS CIRCLES

The logical next step was the institution of the company's Japanese inspired, but none the less home-grown, 'Our Contribution Counts' Circles – designed to 'empower UGC people to make a difference in our crusade for World Class performance.'

The Circles were an enabling mechanism to 'encourage and allow people to get together and form a circle with the aid of a Departmental Facilitator to pursue continuous improvement ideas back in the workplace and to look for ways of resolving problems.'

Type One Circles were set up where a Manager identified an issue, problem or idea he or she wanted evaluated.

Type Two Circles were set up where an employee had an idea for improving the way things are done or a problem he or she would like resolved with the help of colleagues.

Although voluntary, the programme was structured with, for example in the case of Type Two circles, the Facilitator working with the originator of the idea, to consider whether a circle should be formed and, if so, to obtain the permission of line management to proceed.

WHAT'S IN IT FOR ME?

By this time the company had progressed to the enlightened self-interest approach defining the 'What's in it for me?' for employees as 'greater job satisfaction, personal development, fun, enjoyment, creativity, self-confidence, improved personal relationships, development of potential and a sense of achievement that comes from the authority to implement the changes you want to see.'

What's in it for the company? – 'Quite simply the continued growth and prosperity of the business.'

What's in it for the Company? – £2 Million for Starters

What was in it for the Company – apart from an improvement in overall morale – became clear when a pilot circle in the Unipart Industries Division came up with a solution which made a 'non-capable' liquid container 'capable' and saved £30,000 which had been budgeted for a new machine.

Another circle in Oxford persuaded management to hold off on a decision to adopt a Japanese method of stopping water getting into fuel tanks when they were being tested, while they developed a better, simpler and less expensive solution which saved the company around £85,000. Said John, 'There have been immense benefits. So far we have saved £2m.'

The Challenge to Win

Unipart's World Class crusade challenged every individual in the company to research what 'world class' was in their particular area of activity and to achieve it.

'We didn't say, if you are not world class you are an outcast, or you are going to be penalised. We said quite the opposite. If you are doing 10 and world class is 90, and you admit it, you are a hero. We have confidence and trust you to work out how to get to 90 because we believe you want to get there. Now they all have charts on their walls and show me with pride "Look, we are 3 and world class is 10 – and this is what we are doing to get there." People love to win.'

Summary

- A classic case of motivation in action. How Unipart turned a company where workers slept on the job to one in which people 'love to win'.
- How the Unipart motivation effort has evolved with a developing and interlocking system of programmes.
- A QED programme provided ideas-focused lift off.

- Putting People First – introduced the concept of self-awareness, self-esteem and the need for constant development.
- My Contribution Counts – showed each individual ways in which they can make continuous improvements in all aspects of their job with the accent on the need for excellent customer service.
- Mark in Action – recognises and rewards individuals and teams who are pursuing the company goal of 'Outstanding Personal Service'.
- Our Contribution Counts Circles – is the enabling mechanism which encourages and allows people to get together and form circles, with the aid of a departmental 'facilitator' and pursue continuous improvement ideas back in the workplace.
- The crusade for 'World Class' performance is a self-evaluation mechanism which enables employees to match their performance against the world's best in their field and to suggest and put into practice ways in which they can win.

ACTION

- Examine the Unipart Group of Companies' progressive motivation programme.
- Think about what Unipart might be doing for an encore.

14. A Chance to Win – The Renaissance of a Railway

When the driver of a pre-World War Two crack steam train reached his destination, the small boys among the passengers would tip their caps in salute as they walked past the glamorous smut-streaked figure leaning out of his open cab to receive the plaudits that were his due.

As some of the fastest men on earth – 1936 saw the *Mallard* break the world steam record at 126.4 miles an hour – the drivers were a well motivated elite and the vast army of railway employees shared their reflected glory.

It was an 'army' that since 1923 had formed its own proud 'regiments'; the Great Western Railway, the London Midland and Scottish, the London North Eastern Railway and the Southern Railway, all of which generated a fierce and intensely motivating esprit de corps.

Six years of war, however, left the railways with out of date, worn out rolling stock and a war weary workforce for whom 'don't you know there's a war on' had become an automatic response.

In 1948 the Railways were nationalised, after which they were modernised, dieselised and Beeching axed until they finally ran out of steam in 1968.

A Dinosaur Battles with a Legend

As a struggling giant, BR was a soft target for the media, until recently the indecently enthusiastic pall-bearers in waiting for Britain's moribund industries.

Worse still, BR was fighting the legend of the Big Four, a folk memory of fast, punctual trains, smiling porters, luxurious carriages and gourmet meals, a legend firmly fixed in the minds of people who had never experienced the dirty, smelly, uncomfortable Third Class carriages of a neglected branch line. For these reasons and many more – few of them the railwaymens' fault – BR felt that it couldn't win, and it showed.

Motivating a Change

In this climate the most heroic PR efforts backfired or met with monumental disinterest, and even genuine achievements, like the HST world speed record for diesel trains set at 144.7 miles an hour, failed to impress a public who were having difficulty in 'getting there' and had already travelled by air at over twice that speed. However top management noticed, just as they noticed that in 1988 InterCity moved into surplus and a year later made a record run at 162 miles an hour. At last somebody – admittedly having been dealt a better than average hand – seemed to be doing something right.

The Renaissance of the Railways

By 1991, under the Chairmanship of Bob Reid, British Rail had almost completed a re-organisation that divided it into Businesses or 'profit centres' which, while not quite the same as the Big Four with their individual liveries and uniforms, were better than the amorphous BR giant. They had introduced programmes like Quality Through People, the Safety Programme and Organising for Quality and felt able to make statements like 'The renaissance of the railways has begun and the pace will quicken during the coming decade'. British Rail was moving to end a morale problem aggravated by a decade of cost cutting and hostility and was committed to improving safety and quality.

The Best Laid Plans

Susan Hoyle, Assistant Director of Quality for British Rail, remembers the motivating moves of the late 80s and early 90s and the horror of the Clapham disaster of December 12th 1988 in which 35 people were killed and 69 seriously injured. 'It was a dreadful thing to happen to the people involved but to the Railway Industry it was a shock that is still reverberating. Clapham affected morale. Then there was a strike the following year which led to a lot of bitterness.'

Other demotivating factors at that time, she claims, were the perceived hostility of government, the question of privatisation which made many people feel threatened, and an almost invariably hostile press.

The First Step: Identifying the Problem

As all intending motivators must do, BR had begun by identifying the problem – in this case as one of quality.

'The Quality Through People initiative was launched just a couple of weeks before Clapham. It arose out of the fairly obvious fact that we weren't giving people the quality they wanted. We'd been very successful in recognising and controlling our costs but we hadn't been so successful in maintaining our improvement of the quality of what we delivered.

'The service we deliver still isn't good enough – it's not quite as bad as they make out but when we do it really badly you can rely on it getting into the papers. The mistakes of other industries are hidden away but our ghastly mistakes happen when trains fail to arrive at platforms full of people.'

Farewell to Negative KITA – A New Motivating Leadership

The Quality Through People programme launched at the end of 1988 was an acknowledgement that BR had at last realised – or relearned – that it was in the people business. The next stop was to look into new ideas on leadership.

'What we have been working on,' said Susan Hoyle, 'is the concept of the manager as a leader, as a coach. I think we traditionally tended to assume that the manager's job was to know everyone's job better than they did and to kick ass when things went wrong.

'Now, the idea is that the managers are there because they are better at managing people than the other members of the team, who themselves are better at doing their job than he is or she is. The manager's job is to ensure that the other people can do their job properly and can get it right first time.

'Motivational issues, like rewarding and recognition policies are an important tool in enabling the team leader to achieve this and the motivation and morale of our staff is a line responsibility.

Cascading the Message

British Rail employs 135,000 people, so training and remotivating all of them to deliver total quality is a mammoth task; the solution – a series of 'cascaded' courses – is one that can be equally effective for smaller organisations.

The first type of course, each of which lasted a week, was called 'Leadership 500', and was attended by some 780 very senior managers. They then took their teams on the next tranche which was called 'Leadership 5000', which more than 5,000 people attended, after which they took their people on Quality Through Teamwork courses.

Explained Susan, 'The first courses were organised from this office but we are now at the stage at which the final level – called 'Quality at Work' – is being organised within the Businesses and that concerns the people at the sharp end and their supervisors and managers. The people you might see working in travel centres, when you are buying your ticket, the men working on gangs, or the train crews and people like that are just starting to go on these courses.'

THE MESSAGE GETS THROUGH

Early signs that the message was getting through included the abolishing of some obvious 'them' and 'us' symbols, like separate eating arrangements for workers and management, a division that at BR's Headquarters had reached a point at which there were five separate canteens.

'Now there's just one restaurant and the Chief Executive can be seen there regularly, eating with messengers and the rest of the staff', said Susan.

At the same time InterCity had laid down the policy that managers should wear their name badges when travelling on trains, a requirement which applies under the Passengers' Charter to all British Rail Staff who are in contact with the public. InterCity had already realised that a high profile need not be a liability and that turning round a section of an industry in which overall motivation was low could earn more recognition and gratitude than improving an already flourishing and highly motivated business.

A MASTERPIECE OF MOTIVATION

British Rail's *Handbook of Total Quality Management*, in the preparation of which Susan Hoyle played a big part, though devoid of the theatrical element that organisations like Unipart use so effectively, is in many ways a masterpiece of motivation practice.

It begins with a classic example of 'a noble cause' and an exciting vision of 'a thriving industry contributing to the prosperity of the nation', followed by a foreword by Chairman Sir Bob Reid which refers to the 'enormous investment British Rail and its Businesses are making in order to change our culture'.

The next step is a statement of values. BR's Key Values include:

- putting the customer first.
- treating all our people as we would wish them to treat our customers.
- committing to excellence and to continuous improvement.
- encouraging enterprise, initiative and innovation.
- recognising that everyone has a part to play.

Changing the 'WHO?'

Doing this involves changing the way people behave:

- managers need to act as team leaders and role models.
- there was a need to understand the importance of alignment, trust and empowerment.
- there was also a need to move away from the hierarchical approach – which tended not to value fully the contribution of most people – towards a team-based approach which would identify and develop skills throughout the workforce.

Involving to Solve

The importance of teamwork in the management-directed Quality Improvement Process was given particular emphasis in the PSP or Problem Solving Process, with its five steps leading from the identification and understanding of the problem and selecting its likely causes, to analysing alternative solutions, planning action, implementing and monitoring the solution and evaluating the outcome, amending where necessary.

Problem Solving Process techniques used by Quality Improvement Teams include Brainstorming, as a structured method of generating ideas from the entire team, and TPN which assesses the extent – Totally, Partially, or Not at all – to which a specific problem is within the team's control.

'Benchmarking' – like Unipart's World Class campaign –

identifies best possible practice inside or outside BR and provides challenges and goals.

THE MAKING OF A TEAM

Teamwork doesn't happen automatically and BR identify four stages after teams have obtained a management sponsor or 'Champion', checked for duplication of effort, arranged for resources facilities and set in place processes for rewarding success or analysing failure. These are:

- team members overcome suspicion, get to know each other and begin to form attachment to team.
- team members demonstrate friction and resentment as they lay claim to ground and establish pecking order.

NOTE: These are the two stages Major General Grant suggested were obviated by an evident hierarchy.

- team settles down to work, having accepted individual roles and idiosyncrasies.
- team is able to solve problems, seek feedback from team to aid individual development and make decisions.

Interestingly, adding new members to the team sets back the team-building process.

THE COST OF GETTING IT WRONG

Committed gung-ho motivators may take issue with BR who, having identified 'the cost of getting it right' – items like prevention, training and appraisal – include, in 'the cost of getting it wrong', not only waste but also the factor of exceeding customer requirements; i.e. devoting time and resources to products and services which exceed what the customer expects and what the customer will therefore pay for. Received opinion in most highly motivated companies is that giving the external and internal customer more than they expect, and providing service 'above the call of duty', ensures customer loyalty and is motivating in itself.

However, British Rail deal in billions and, for the moment at any rate, are spending our money, so most of us would be happy to see them get things exactly right. To do more than is necessary *here* while failing abysmally *there* is a misuse of resources. As the handbook puts it, for British Rail the cost of getting it right is measured in millions of pounds. The cost of getting it wrong is likely to be close to £1bn a year.

Send the Rolls!

From the outset BR make it clear that 'Quality', as used by quality practitioners, is a precise term, and cite the example that in normal speech a Rolls Royce is a 'quality' vehicle which is 'very expensive, luxurious and glamorous'.

Quality practitioners would call it a 'high grade car' and before agreeing to call it a Quality car would want to know the purpose for which the user wanted it. In these terms, a Rolls Royce is not a quality car if what you have in mind is racing along the beach. If on the other hand what you want is a well-furnished mobile office which will impress the neighbours, then the Rolls would probably qualify as Quality. The example illustrates a fundamental difference of approach and one which is entirely understandable when laying down the ground rules for a major investment of public funds.

However, it is possible to achieve an enormous amount of positive motivation by providing more than people expect, by 'sending the Rolls' – not every day of course, but on the occasions that people will remember for the rest of their lives.

Everyone Remembers a Touch of Class

We all remember the times when people have surprised and delighted us by doing more for us than we expected. Twenty-five years on, for example, it is still possible to recall the names of the French Hilton Manager who had champagne and a bowl of fruit sent to one's room, or the captain of a light cruiser who rescheduled the Arctic 'Officer of the Watch' manoeuvres of his tiny flotilla 'so you can see the whole of the tax money you will ever pay spent in one fell swoop'.

Note that you couldn't possibly buy these things, any more than you could buy an unexpected civic reception in Scarborough or the gesture of a self-made millionaire who really did send the Rolls Royce to pick up an eighteen month old child because 'a smaller car might make her car sick.'

Memorable events are great motivation and, in fact, one of the highly motivated companies we looked at (Chapter 19) really does send a Rolls Royce for a month to its winning team.

Very properly the upper echelons of British Rail are concentrating for the moment on getting it right, but there are already signs that, closer to the sharp end, they could well be thinking of the motivational effects of service beyond the call of duty symbolised by – 'sending the Rolls.'

DON'T RUN ROUND IN CIRCLES

If you are to get the most out of 'quality', or any other kind of motivating circles, the effort has to be properly structured and monitored. BR's Tracking System, an on-line database of areas under study, shows how this can be done.

The Index Input Document records for each Quality Improvement Team: an index number, a responsibility code, a subject keyword, subject detail, the name of circle leader, circle phone number, start date-finish date, the number of people involved and a coded 'scope of benefit' ranging from 0 to £250,000.

CALCULATING RESULTS

Results of any initiative of this sort are calculated first on the number and quality of ideas received. Here BR scored well on both counts with 493 teams operating over a period of two years. About 200 of them had either achieved or were on course for a benefit of more than £250,000.

All were motivating in the way they involved people and many addressed specifically motivational topics concerning morale and environment. Examples included 'improve environment at Bristol Bath Road', 'A project on lineside tidiness', and 'Replacement of an obsolete form by new signing-on sheet'.

Although the project had not yet been 'cascaded' to the footplate and platform there was plenty of evidence of a 'Theory Y' rather than a 'Theory X' workforce.

Ever Decreasing Circles

TOP MANAGEMENT SHOULD BE AWARE THAT THE REQUIREMENT TO GET IT RIGHT FIRST TIME APPLIES TO THEM AS MUCH AS ANYONE ELSE – PERHAPS EVEN MORE. The law of diminishing returns applies to many types of effort and in the case of BR there were indications in their house publications that some middle managers, though prepared to give their all once again, were hopeful that the latest campaign would be the definitive effort.

However the same magazines and staff newspapers showed that there was great loyalty and some splendid motivation at grass roots level, including knock-ons from previous campaigns, good response to cash reward incentive schemes, genuine pride in achievement, involvement as a workplace group in charitable causes – both in-house and outside – involvement in 'noble cause' type adventures, Outward Bound style courses and workplace based sports events.

The Passengers' Charter

Another BR initiative, the Passengers' Charter – this time government mandated – received a surprisingly good initial reception from the press who, unlike the Consumer Association, were – as the anti-BR *Sun* put it – 'not prepared to find them guilty without a trial'.

Many journalists focused on the 'stick' motivation, calling for BR to provide compensation, refunds and discounts in cases of sub-standard performance.

Most rail staff, though cynical about the pre-election timing, agreed with managers like John Nelson the MD of Network South-East that 'knowing what we are expected to achieve – what *is* winning – will help individual men and women working for this railway to understand what contribution they can make.'

WINNING

British Rail have a long way to go before small boys once again begin queuing up to become engine drivers, but apart from the money benefits, which have been considerable, their initiatives are paying dividends. For instance if you have been out of the country for any length of time you will notice that trains are more punctual, carriages cleaner and staff more efficient and friendlier than, say, five years ago.

In Susan Hoyle's words British Rail's motivation initiatives are earning them 'a chance to win.'

SUMMARY

- What happened to the once proud Railway Companies and how they became a target for often unfair media attacks.
- The 'renaissance of the railways'; can a structured motivation campaign grab the hearts and minds of 135,000 people in such a way as to channel their undoubted loyalty and enthusiasm?
- 'Cascading' the message from company Chairman to carriage cleaner.

- Why BR is keen not to waste your money by either getting things wrong – or by getting things 'too right'.
- How to plan, form and monitor 'quality' and other motivating circles.

ACTION

- Write down – if you are old enough – anything you remember about Rail travel in the days of the legendary Big Four. You probably won't remember waiting for hours on Crewe Station – once a very different kind of legend – but you will recall with ease any piece of outstanding service.
- Try the same exercise for BR. You may not remember having been among the 762m passengers, most of whose 16,040 trains were clean and punctual, but you will remember any unpunctuality, surliness or bad service.

15. The Case of the Lady Driver

Not many managers have the resources of British Rail but, there again, not many of them number their workforce in tens of thousands, have motivation problems that go back to the First World War or are forced to operate under the vigilant eyes of the press.

However, most managers, whatever the size of their operation, are already motivating to some extent, even if many of them have only a vague notion of why they are doing what they do.

Their problem is how to go about improving the motivation of their organisation and increasing the productivity of their people – by, among other things, making sure they enjoy their work.

Rebecca Jenkins, the 31 year old Manager Director of Lane Group plc, took over the leadership of the company three years ago, fired with the determination to fulfil both those main aims.

Her success story is a classic of motivation in action in a medium-sized business.

THE DYNAMIC KNOWLEDGEABLE LEADER

Rebecca is the ideal person to motivate a transport company. She has already done virtually every job in the organisation herself, including the key job of driving a truck. As the holder of an LGV licence she is well on the way to overcoming most of the 'them' and 'us' barriers that might otherwise have been even worse than usual for a woman boss in a man's world.

Looking for an opportunity

After taking a hotel management course at Brunel College, and working for Holiday Inns for three years, Rebecca decided that her rarity value as a woman would give her the edge in a transport company. 'At the age of 21 I decided to do something different and get an LGV licence.

'I took a holiday from my hotel work and, after passing my licence at the minimum age, decided that having spent so much money I should go to work at it immediately.

'I joined what was then Peter Lane Transport and after doing multi-drop distribution work around the country decided to try for a management position again. There was a job going in sales and by that time the transport bug had got to me. I thought it was exciting being involved in distributing materials for industry.'

Having an Aim

I knew what I wanted to do in the company – which was to reach management level – and from Sales Rep I moved to Sales Manager, then to Marketing Director. Three years ago I became Managing Director, which gave me the opportunity to put my ideas into action, but even before that motivation and the need for constant improvement had always been at the forefront of my thoughts.'

Without being a theoretician Rebecca realised instinctively the need for 'NET motivation in the desired direction.'

'The objectives I have for the company have to be shared by everybody, otherwise I've got 250 employees who could all pull in different directions. If every one of them is not aware of what senior management are hoping to achieve, and expect to achieve, it isn't any good.'

A MOTIVATED WORKFORCE FULFILS THE PROMISES OF MANAGEMENT

Rebecca pointed out that unless all of the drivers, for example, were aware that she wanted to provide a top quality level of service for the customers she would not be able to achieve it.

'If I tell a major Mail Order Company, what our drivers will do and describe their high standards of efficiency and politeness, it's all totally pointless if our driver doesn't operate to those high standards, either because he doesn't know we want him to, doesn't know why we want him to or doesn't know how.

'Management have got to communicate throughout the company and we work extremely hard at that.'

MOTIVATION BY 'CAFETERIA' JOB ASSIGNMENT

When Rebecca took over there was no corporate policy on motivation – with the exception of the sales force – so she was forced to start from scratch.

Her first major problem, and one which faces many managers, is that some of the jobs on offer were frankly boring and she knew that it would be difficult to generate excitement.

'I knew from experience that it is normal to get two main types of driver – the ones who get a kick out of doing a different job every day with new routes and new people and the others who really love going up and down the same old road, leaving at the same time, meeting the same people and getting back at the same time.

'What we do is quite simple. We try to find out what the drivers want and what they like to do and set the jobs round them. It doesn't always work but that is our aim and intention and all the drivers know that.'

CHANGING THE WORKING ENVIRONMENT

'We've spent money on site improvements, in which the staff has a major input, and we also implement staff suggestions in non-profit making areas, for example placing re-cycling bins around the building and bins for empty soft drink cans and so on.'

Staff get a say in choosing the equipment they will use. Recently the drivers chose the design and colour of their own uniform; they are currently being asked to help with ideas for choosing the new corporate livery and, as the people most affected by truck design and construction, they will have a big share in deciding what vehicles the company will acquire to augment its 150 strong fleet.

INVOLVING TO SOLVE

In spite of being a committed motivator, dedicated to the principle of involving to solve, the MD of Lane Group plc keeps the reins in her hands.

'What we have are "Teamwork" meetings. We have representatives elected by the employees and every month the representative and the warehouse office get together so that they can discuss any issues in the company. Minutes of the meeting are then put on the notice board and the staff are entitled to have an answer to any of the points they have raised – by the next meeting.'

As well as 'Teamwork' meetings the company also publishes a Teamwork magazine once every three months, for which it encourages, and receives, critical contributions from staff and drivers.

'In addition to this, all employees are given a regular update on everything that is going on in the company. We've been working on this for the last three years and we are constantly improving on it.'

MOTIVATING BY LISTENING

'One thing I like to do,' says Rebecca, 'is listen to any of our staff who have ideas for improvement.'

Listening pays dividends. One member of Lane's traffic office staff recently came up with an idea for a trunking operation between each of the firm's depots. 'The idea was to send a loaded vehicle at night into our centre in Birmingham so that if you had, say, a box of stationery that you wanted to get from Bristol to Leeds overnight you could put it on our trunk system and it would get there.

'We thought this sounded good and decided to give it a try and it has now been running for six months with utilisation currently running at ninety five per cent.'

Motivating by Increased Responsibility

'We are passing responsibility down the line. Depot managers are virtually running their own businesses. They are responsible for putting their budget together and are totally accountable.

'It's based over 12 months and the first time people were putting budgets together they were a bit concerned about making a prediction 12 months ahead and how they could forecast it. Now it's all been polished up and is working well.'

Rebecca wanted to make the managers' jobs more stimulating by making them more accountable and involved.

The Bottom Line – Quantifying the Results of Motivation

The acid test for managers who are themselves accountable is to ask: 'Is my motivation effort producing quantifiable results? Is it making the company a better organisation for people to work for and is that working to produce better quality service for the customer and better profits for the organisation?'

In Rebecca Jenkins' case the answer is an unequivocal 'Yes.' Said Rebecca, 'The staff make their own discipline although they still have to be aware of the guidelines and the framework in which they have to operate. We have very few problems with lateness or absenteeism.

'Our staff turnover is currently 1.5 per cent compared with an industry wide average of just over five per cent and we have achieved an increase of productivity of 50 per cent over the last 12 months to reach an annual turnover of £13m.

'Motivation has been responsible for about 80 per cent of the increase because people are responsible for their own divisions and are really focused on them. It shows that motivation really works.'

WHAT ABOUT THE WORKERS?

Lane's operate a profit share scheme with a percentage share in the profit for the financial year for all their staff, including drivers, and everyone is encouraged to have shares in the company. Wages are in line with the industry average and keep pace with inflation.

MOTIVATING FOR THE FUTURE

To help Lane's motivate for the future Rebecca has appointed 31 year old Diane Farrell as Communications Manager.

Diane explained: 'We have suggestion schemes in all our depots and I'm finding that, for instance, the Bristol depot is putting four or five suggestions a week through the lines. Not all of them can be actioned, but if they look as though they will affect the organisation we will take them a step further, sit down with the driver, get all the feedback possible from him and then talk it over at managerial level and see what we can do. The driver will receive payment and then over the next 12 months, he will get a percentage of additional savings or profits.

'We will listen to anything; it doesn't have to have a direct financial benefit but it has to improve the organisation.'

MINOR MOTIVATIONS

Some of the motivating factors at Lane's are apparently trivial but they are signs of what both Rebecca and Diane term a 'happy company'. For example, everyone including the boss is on first name terms, and everybody has a say in company events.

... And Major Ones

Nobody who is totally happy driving a truck is forced to change, but opportunities are there and all vacancies are announced on staff notice boards. The policy of the company is to recruit for potential wherever possible.

Training, though seen as a motivator, has so far been largely practical, but the company is already in Europe and hopes soon to move in with its own vehicles, so language classes, proposed by a member of staff are planned for next year.

Motivating for Results

A pragmatic approach to driver training means that drivers are assessed on their driving ability once a year. 'If a driver meets certain criteria,' says Rebecca, 'by always arriving at work on time, keeping his vehicle clean, wearing his uniform and not giving rise to any customer complaints, he can apply for upgrading. Top graded drivers have an above average salary, family medical insurance and improved company pension contributions. If they don't perform, obviously they can be downgraded, but the incentive to be upgraded is there.'

Drivers are also investigated by Training Force, the company's in-house training unit, after which an advisor comes in for a meeting with about six or seven of them at a time – a driving seminar, following which the advisor goes out with individual drivers to show them how they can improve their driving. The instructor is there to make suggestions rather than to give orders and there's no grading at the end of the course.

Motivating for Efficiency

The training is an example of motivation bringing tangible results. Said Diane Farrell, 'The drivers enjoy the courses which are "events" and the cost per driver is £150. On the average vehicle, based on 50,000 miles per annum, by correct gear changing, braking and so on, the driver improves fuel consumption by one mile per gallon, that is, from 11 to 12 miles which can save £650 per year – every year.

'So far in real terms our well motivated drivers have made an overall saving of 10 per cent, resulting in a saving of £100,000 on our £1m annual fuel bill.'

TRAINING PROGRAMMES FOR ALL

Lane's management is highly visible. This year, for example, the company is running a Customer Care training programme for everyone in the company and that means that Rebecca and her management team will attend courses along with the drivers.

'The drivers are learning about Customer Care on the road, how to drive sensibly and how their actions will affect profitability.

'We haven't done anything in terms of outside study courses for our employees in the past, in the sense of combining outside study with work, but it is something we are looking into.'

CARING AND THE CAS RATIO

Rebecca is proud of running a happy and successful company. 'We are delighted at some of the comments our people make. They are definitely enjoying the challenges and satisfactions of their jobs and having fun. I think most of them share my motivation which is based largely on a desire to make the company tremendously successful – for everyone.' Rebecca unhesitatingly put the company's CAS Ratio at 75 per cent carrot and 25 per cent stick. 'We can accept mistakes if people have had the courage to have a go,' she says, and her one regret is that the company currently employs only one woman truck driver. 'It's a great shame. We are an equal opportunity organisation. If a woman comes up and she's more capable of doing the job than a man, then she's the one with the job.'

A MOTIVATING MODEL

Lane's could well serve as a model of a solid and effective middle of the road structured motivation style company, with nothing too flamboyant about it, but with most elements in place and a steady progression in the direction of the Pleasure Principle, based firmly on a healthy proportion of enlightened self interest.

Relating theory to practice, there is an acceptance of the importance of money, with the accent on employee participation achieved by rewarding individual achievement and by profit sharing.

Environmental factors including decor, equipment and machinery are taken care of.

Induction packages, conducted tours and universal use of first names make employees feel more than just 'cogs' by emphasising the caring 'family atmosphere'.

Job satisfaction is increased by 'horses for courses' job assignments and by involvement of employees at all levels in some of the decision making processes.

Empowerment has reached middle management and will no doubt progress downwards, while employees seeking self-actualisation have genuine opportunities to develop their potential. Perhaps of equal importance, because of Rebecca's driving background, anyone who is happy to remain a driver need have little fear that he or she will be undervalued.

This style of motivation is suited to a strong and totally self-confident manager in a business which is still small enough for him or her to know each employee personally.

SUMMARY

- Case study of medium-sized company in which a strong, charismatic leader has consciously employed motivation techniques to produce 'a NET movement in the desired direction' which in this example included a £7.5m rise in annual turnover.

- Three years of successful practical motivation has culminated inthe appointment of a Communications Manager with special responsibility for motivation.
- The company's motivation shows classic Maslow progression but, although managers are being given increasing autonomy and empowered to 'run their own show', top management remains firmly, if less obviously, in charge of overall strategy.

ACTION

- Compare your own organisation with the one described. Is there any opportunity for constructive 'swiping'?
- Rebecca Jenkins the MD has been working for three years on the question of updating all employees on 'things that are going on in the company' and has still not found a totally satisfactory way of doing this. Can you suggest a possible answer to the problem? (One suggestion is given in the next chapter.)

16. Motivating in the Public Sector

One or two managers who have read this far, especially those who come into direct daily contact with the sharp end, may be beginning to think that any motivation other than the threat of the sack on the one hand and an extra couple of quid in the pay packet on the other would not work for their people.

'It's all very well,' they could be thinking, 'for young men running the family business, for big company top brass with unlimited budgets, for intellectuals insulated from reality by batallions of executives, or for MDs whose employees are happy to play a "highly motivated" role, provided the money is right.

'They don't come into contact with the sort of workers we first line managers have to deal with.

'In our world, many employees are not so much Theory X people as Theory XXXX people, whose aim is to do as little as possible for as much money as they can get. Motivation just wouldn't work on them.'

THE CHAMELEON WHO?

Of course many managers above the rank of supervisor stand little chance of meeting the real WHO? because their authority and their invisible uniform of affluence, accent and manner tend to turn what ought to be a meeting between human beings into yet another confrontation between 'them' and 'us'.

In the same way, senior managers in, say, the Department of

Health and Social Security rarely meet the awkward "customers" with whom their juniors have to deal, but are confronted instead by people rendered docile and conciliatory by the presence of a 'boss'.

ALMOST EVERYONE CAN BE MOTIVATED

The fact is – and this is why we have stressed two World Wars in which millions of men and women from geniuses to dullards were motivated to perform incredible feats and make unbelievable sacrifices – almost everyone can be motivated by factors other than money. However, for managers who are not in a position to hire the best, train the rest and get rid of the pest, and whose employees are prisoners of their 'culture', it may not always seem that way.

MOTIVATING IN LOCAL GOVERNMENT – THE LEWISHAM EXPERIENCE

Tony Lear is a local government Director of Environmental Services who, after a fifteen year stint with the London Borough of Lewisham, has moved to the London Borough of Brent who hired him specifically to repeat his motivation success.

Tony, who took a 'temporary' job in local government straight from school, got into mainstream management in the early 1980s when the government introduced competition into local authority services. It was, he asserts, a revolution in public service management which made local authorities become more businesslike and professional in their approach. 'I ran the Building Works Division from 1984–1989 and then spent three years as Director of Environmental Services, so I really do know about motivating people on the ground.'

THE LIMITATIONS OF MONEY

Tony remembers all too vividly the 'awful Prices and Incomes Board time in the 1960s when motivation was seen as purely a financial thing which real experience showed to be absolute nonsense. People were highly motivated to fiddle the scheme rather than to do the job properly, and that went on right through the 1970s during which absenteeism and poor timekeeping, poor morale, and a high turnover of staff were the norm.

'People were coming to work but all they were interested in was filling in their time. If a customer came to them with a problem they didn't care sufficiently to tackle it, so they just fobbed the customer off. "It's not my job, not my problem – it's somebody elses."'

PRISONERS OF THE SYSTEM

Tony remembers that as a newcomer he was horrified to discover that managers either got out, or learned to play the system and how to achieve a position of power in it – an occupation which demanded all their energy and enthusiasm.

'Everybody from refuse collectors to clerks and administrators was absolutely "turned off" and they were using their energy and efforts to beat the system rather than to improve it.'

THE LOOK BUSY CULTURE

At the London Borough of Kensington and Chelsea – never known as a particularly inefficient organisation – Tony worked in a section of about 30 people who had virtually nothing to do. 'We were told to keep our heads down and "look busy" if anyone passed by, because the managers didn't want it to be seen that we had no work to do.'

Some people in Local Government – like the dustman who was so fed up with finishing work at 10.30 every morning that he drifted along to Leyton Orient Football Club where he became an award winning groundsman – left their jobs rather than endure the boredom.

THE NEED TO MOTIVATE

The decision of the Thatcher regime to make local government compete with the private sector, and to demonstrate that they were providing value for money, made the need for motivation imperative.

'In the early 1980s I got involved with Building Works – an organisation of 700–800 whose main task was to maintain Lewisham's 40,000 dwellings, its housing stock. The government were saying that we were going to have the tender for work and win it in competition, but the reality was that the service we were providing was absolute rubbish.

'Tenants in Lewisham would have welcomed anyone else coming in to do the work because we were defending jobs and services that quite frankly weren't worth defending. We had to improve service, we had to improve productivity and we had to change working practices away from the old demarcation areas.

'The old financial bonus schemes had failed, the old style heavy handed management had failed. We had to do something – we had to motivate.'

THE HIERARCHY OF BUILDING WORKERS

Said Tony, 'At the time I knew about motivation theory but there's a lot of difference between theory and practice.

'Take the Hierarchy of Needs. I was managing an organisation of building workers who were quite well paid, certainly better than most of their colleagues in the industry. Not only that, but they had a guarantee of 52 weeks employment a year which no one else had. In fact they had all the basics, including security, and many of them were becoming owner occupiers. Unfortunately, it didn't follow naturally that they then wanted to improve their skills or enrich their jobs, quite the reverse.

'I found they became obsessed with defending the bottom layers of the "Hierarchy" Pyramid. In fact, a lot of their efforts went into finding ways to enhance their pay by doing private jobs on Council time.'

MOTIVATION AND THE 'FOOT SOLDIERS'

At the time, the corporate thinking about motivation was demonstrably in advance of the 'culture' of the WHO? Their ideas, says Tony, were based on power sharing and the feeling that in a highly unionised environment, like the building trade, everything would be all right if you could involve the unions in the way the Europeans do.

'Lewisham wasn't ready for that and it just didn't work, even though the unions we involved were quite positive about it.

'The big lesson for me, at the time, was that you can have all the consultation you like but, at the end of the day, someone – the manager – has to make up his or her mind and take the risk, and get the credit if it goes right and the reverse if it goes wrong.

'It all boils down to telling Fred to get on with the job and the difficulty lies in getting people to go along with your decision.'

THE NEED FOR LEADERSHIP

Tony was 'amazed' to find that people wanted a set of rules and that while a workforce was not like a group of children they needed to know how far they could go and to know that, if they were asking for something, the manager was at some point going to say 'No'.

'The corporate approach was based on the belief that you could manage the big batallions by involving the workforce in the decision making process in a big way, but in reality very little of that got down to the foot soldiers who were just as disempowered as they had ever been.'

CHANGING THE WHO?

However, the WHO?, with its deeply entrenched 'them' and 'us' attitudes, was changing, albeit slowly, and imposed financial restraints gave local government a chance to speed up the process, not by mass sackings, but by saying like Field Marshal Montgomery: 'If you don't want to be a party to the way we are going to do things we can talk about amicable ways of your getting out of the organisation.'

Lewisham has knocked £20 million off its budget in the last three years and has lost 10 per cent of its staff in the last 15 months, providing some of what Harvey-Jones calls 'the opportunities presented by managing in a recession.'

There has been what Tony calls 'a massive clear-out of people' and, since the ones who remained were not usually those on a pre-ordained collision course with management, they were generally more responsive to motivation. Nevertheless, like everyone else, they were the creatures of their conditioning, which was not such as to make them totally receptive to management initiatives.

MOTIVATING 'JACK THE LAD'

Says Tony, 'The workforce I had to motivate was not only predominantly blue collar but people who saw themselves as the aristocrats of blue collar: the building workers, the electricians and the plumbers. Most of them were also pretty wayward characters in many ways – your typical Cockney "Jack the Lad".

'With that sort of character you can't go from the Stone Age to the Jet Age of motivation in one jump. If you have a history of not involving people, and of telling people that you are not interested in what they think, you can't go to the other extreme overnight and tell them that you want their involvement or that you are going to empower them – because all you're going to get is scepticism.'

BRINGING IN THE PROFESSIONALS

Tony needed to involve his workers and arouse their enthusiasm if he was to persuade them to make full use of their evident expertise. His answer was to bring in an outside motivation consultancy in the hope that it would help him overcome workers' scepticism. He decided on an 'ideas' based campaign and first checked the current state of Lewisham's traditional suggestion schemes.

He discovered that the Accounts Department had been running a suggestions scheme for ten years with 'virtually no take up at all', while in Building Works there had been five ideas in eight years and 'nobody knew what had happened to them.'

'No wonder I thought the consultant from IML was being optimistic when he talked about 75 to 80 per cent co-operation but in fact we did get that.'

Using Humour

Humour is an extremely useful motivational tool which releases tension and helps allay fears and counter conditioning.

'It was humour that helped us to make the bridge,' said Tony. 'In fact some of the Union shop stewards became leading lights in the campaign because they enjoyed the humour.

'The fact that the prizes had little intrinsic value helped the fun element to emerge. If you are offering people £500 or £2,000 for their ideas, a lot of people who have ideas think that you are only interested in the big stuff, and there's no point in them putting up their idea.

'With giving mugs what we had was a very loose, "let's all have a go, maybe I can put in an idea today, who hasn't got a mug?" approach.'

The Case of the Sceptical Shop Steward

Not everyone was won over immediately. 'We had one steward who was an absolute misery and always looked on the black side. He came to me right at the start and said "You're only giving us mugs. It's a bloody silly idea; a waste of time."

'A few weeks into the campaign he knocked on my door and I thought, "Here we go again", but he told me, "I was in the van the other day and I came up with one of the ideas I've had for improvement and a bloke in the van nicked it. He's got a mug for my idea!"

The Breakthrough

'That was a straw in the wind. Most people appeared to like the campaign and were entering into the spirit of it, but one supervisor decided he'd had enough and declared that talking to his workers every morning and getting their ideas was taking up too much time and he wasn't going to do it any more.

'It was then that, not I or any of the managers, but the first line supervisors all turned round and told him that talking to workers was what management was all about and that he should have been doing it anyway. It really just took off in that way.'

. . . and the Follow Up

Tony Lear followed up the success of the QED motivation campaign by asking everyone in the organisation to come up with a programme for improving their service throughout the year.

'People have been coming up with a total of around 150 improvement initiatives and we are getting a 98 per cent achievement rate with 146 to 147 ideas implemented, which is fantastic. Last year we launched a guarantee scheme for our refuse collections, promising to pay the customers £1 – the cost of two weeks' collection – if we hadn't collected their bin on the day we said we would. We do 4.2m collections a year and out of the first 3m we paid £1 back 53 times. Fifty three service failures out of 3m – it's fantastic.'

When Success is Telling People who you Work for

The real measure of Tony Lear's success, and one which has amazed Tony himself, is that his people now have pride in their jobs, themselves and their organisation.

'In local government when you go to a party on Saturday night and people ask where you work you usually tell a lie or at the very least duck the question. Now people will say that they work for The

London Borough of Lewisham and say it in such a way as to challenge anyone to put them down.'

Of course, the people Tony now talks of as 'having ownership of the problem' are basically the same WHO? as those who once devoted most of their energies to fiddling the system, just as he is the same chap who once put his head down and pretended to be busy. Motivation does make a difference.

THE WORTHING WAY

As might be expected, the Health Authority at Worthing in Sussex did not have many of the problems encountered by Tony Lear on the building sites of a South London Borough.

As in most National Health Service organisations there was in Worthing a tradition dating from Victorian times of care, hard work and a sense of vocation. Other traditions, like the superiority and infallibility of the medical profession, and the assumption that the obedience of devoted workers would be unquestioning and total – though perhaps less evident in Worthing than some other areas – were inappropriate to the new WHO? many of whom considered that their willingness to serve was being exploited.

In fact the British National Health Service is probably as good an example as any of the Law of Diminishing Returns applied to motivation, in as much as the totally genuine motivation of the 'Noble Cause' was used as the near universal answer to staff requests for improvement in pay and conditions. However the satisfactions provided by giving service to others do not pay mortgages, or buy children's food or holidays and throughout the Health Service this feeling of malaise was exacerbated by financial cut-backs and a tarnished public image.

DON'T THROW OUT THE BABY WITH THE BATHWATER

At Worthing, as Training Services Director Mrs Wendy White made clear, it was essential not to throw out the good things from the past but to build on good practice.

In fact when Worthing began to motivate towards total quality in 1989 they were building not only on tradition but on an initiative called The Worthing Way launched some three years earlier.

Said Wendy, 'We called in Denis Walker, who had worked for British Airways and is now a consultant on management and quality issues, and other consultants to deliver local management development programmes of which motivation is a key component.

'We ran a workshop called Quality Leadership and Change for our managers who are responsible for the motivation of their staff, which enabled them to get together and look at the challenges facing them and then go back and involve their staff.

'The result has been great enthusiasm and great teamwork, particularly in the Health Centre and the Hospital.'

MOTIVATION DOESN'T MEAN SPENDING A LOT OF MONEY

One thing the Worthing Health Authority and the Lewisham builders had in common was that money was tight, but this can stimulate the flow of ideas.

'One of the early lessons for us,' said Wendy, 'was that if you make some improvement in the environment you start to unlock a lot of ideas. They don't have to be major things. It could be for example that a desk is in the wrong place and people have been walking round it for years. Simply moving the desk can make a difference and perhaps lead to the re-organisation of the whole office and its working practices. It was the same in the wards where a bit of decoration or the introduction of duvets and covers was a terrific boost to getting more improvement ideas from staff.'

IMPROVING SELF-ESTEEM

The idea was to introduce a dress code for Health Centre receptionist staff who now wear a particular colour and conform to a standard which gives them a corporate identity.

Two areas in the hospitals which were suffering from low self-esteem were the porters and domestics. Here, name changes to 'Portering Services' and 'Housekeeping Services' were part of the motivation effort and they have been issued with smart new uniforms. 'They seem happy and the evidence is that they are talking more with the staff on the wards and contributing to the process.'

THE CASE OF THE MOTIVATED CARETAKER

As in Lewisham, Involving to Solve has resulted in some surprising individual changes in attitude. 'The teams we have set up have been multi-levelled as well as multi-disciplined, so that people at all levels are being given an opportunity to contribute to the process.

'For example, perhaps one of the most dynamic members of the Health Centre team was the caretaker. Traditionally in the Health Service the Caretaker is a man you ring up with a request, knowing that with luck he may get around to it in about four hours.

'This chap got so involved that his contribution to the project was phenomenal and he became a specialist in breaking down barriers and getting things done.'

CHALLENGE

Hospitals are places in which an already dedicated workforce has occasionally to be motivated to provide services which are beyond anything normally required in industry, and one example of this comes from Scotland where Brian Lord, before going into Health Education, was a Nursing Officer in a large psychiatric hospital.

Psycho-geriatric Wards are not particularly joyous places to work in and Brian discovered that things were being made worse because many of the patients in one particular ward were suffering from bed sores.

'At the time a new treatment had become available but the nurses simply were not using it. I decided to motivate by challenge and example. I had photographs taken of each bed sore, put them up on the notice board and told the staff that our challenge was to reduce them to nil.

'I also put on a white coat and gave them a hand in administering the treatment and within three months almost all of the photographs had been removed from the board.'

THE RIPPLE EFFECT

Brian was surprised to discover that he had solved more than the original problem. 'Because the nurses had successfully faced one challenge, new curtains and a new floor covering were asked for and obtained and these had a positive effect on the morale of staff and patients.

'Other wards in the unit providing similar care noticed the changes and at their unit meetings staff began to exchange ideas and to motivate each other. This in turn put pressure on unit and other managers to respond to staff initiatives at ward level. As a result the standard of patient care and staff morale both took an upwards turn.'

As is the case with many motivation efforts, the ripple effects were still going on long after the problem that provided the original motivating impetus had been solved.

SUMMARY

- Motivation in a public sector with the Victorian legacy.

(1) The Lewisham Experience. The problems of motivating a workforce with a tradition of 'featherbedding', apathy, time wasting, and beating the system – and that was just the managers.

- How leadership, a change in the WHO? brought about by a

change in 'culture' and accelerated by a chance to 'get rid of the pests', made a motivation initiative possible.
- How an appeal to Cockney humour and genuine involvement resulted in a 'Fifty Three' service failures in 3m dustbin collections' triumph and new pride for the workforce.

(2) The Worthing Way. Worthing decides to build on past traditions of service and good practice with a Total Quality approach. How small motivations made a big difference and how involvement turned a caretaker – a Health Service job synonymous with the leisurely and obstructive approach – into a co-operative human dynamo.

(3) Scotland – the ripple effect of motivating the solution to a specific problem and how it changed the attitude of first a ward – then a hospital.

ACTION

- Check on any small motivating moves you might be able to make without spending any money. You might find, like Worthing Health Authority, that you could make a motivating change in the workplace environment by doing something as simple as moving an inconveniently sited desk.
- Install a mental bell which will ring every time you hear Victorian phrases like; 'We've always done it that way'; 'It was good enough for Mr James'; or 'You can't expect people of that sort to think for themselves.'

17. Motivating by Events

Managers who have motivated their main people, inspired their supervisors and sold their salespeople on a triple target initiative, could still find themselves with a motivation problem, namely: 'How can I make a boring job interesting?'

The answer is quite simple – 'You can't.'

However, there are things you can do to improve matters for the men or women who are beginning to feel that they are taking part in a Chaplin movie in which the machines are gaining on them.

One of these is to automate the problem out of existence, but this is expensive and could leave some workers out of a job.

A CHANGE IS AS GOOD . . .

Another answer is switching jobs every now and again. We are not talking here about multi-skilling but of exchanging tasks, almost like the bread slicer we heard of who said he relieved the monotony of his job by 'moving to the other side.'

Another palliative measure is to seek out for such work those people who prefer to put themselves on 'automatic' and free their brains for other activities like chatting, listening to music and so on. Managers who do this should make sure they provide opportunities for those people with drive and potential to leave stultifying repetitive work and move on to something else. Not to do this could lead to a waste of human resources. Music can certainly reduce boredom levels, while environmental changes like quietening machines – cotton workers for instance used to have to lip read – can make jobs more tolerable, as can a good canteen and rest room facilities and the like. However, a routine job will remain a routine job.

MAKING EVENTS HAPPEN

Most good motivators, whether managers or motivation consultants, have something of the showman about them, and a well staged motivation campaign is very much an 'EVENT' which brings humour, colour and fun into the workplace. At the same time it involves everyone and fulfils a serious motivating role in overcoming inertia, often with near miraculous results.

EVENTS ARE MEMORABLE

There was a time when events were the prerogative of management, who in many cases rewarded themselves and senior colleagues for their efforts on behalf of the company with, say, a day at the races or a tent at Henley, usually combined with a PR initiative. Such events, while motivating for those concerned, perhaps did rather less for those employees who were left behind.

Now, however, the 'EVENTS' idea is cascading right down to the shop floor and general office, so that everyone can not only enjoy the occasion but also derive a feeling of involvement and of being allowed to share in some of the 'perks' of the enterprise.

A BIT OF A DO

Office parties can be a disaster, but concerns like Lane's Transport use Christmas to motivate by having their 'officers' serve Christmas dinner to the troops.

Again, events are frequently used to focus attention on motivational recognition, in the form of ceremonies like InterCity's Excellence Award Lunches, where the Director John Prideaux invites winners of silver lapel pins, including conductors, drivers and storemen, to join him for lunch aboard a floating five-star restaurant.

Some events can be even more elaborate, like the glitzy all-dancing, all-singing Epcot launch of Unipart as a private company, which involved everyone in the firm and is still on record as a much borrowed video.

THE TOYOTA INITIATIVE

In 1991 Toyota GB Ltd. decided to take initiatives to ensure the continued involvement and commitment of their staff. Personnel Director Alan Dawson, with 400 employees and 4,500 people in the dealer network to motivate, ran a successful motivation campaign for Toyota (GB) staff which produced 2,500 ideas, many of which have been implemented.

The campaign also inspired one idea which could run and run, when Toyota decided to involve everyone in the launch of their new Carina. Said Alan, 'We staged a big product launch and invited all our staff along so that everyone not only saw for themselves what the company was doing but was able to visit another location and appreciate that they were part of a large and successful organisation.'

EVENTS CAN BE SMALL

Events need not be world-shaking to be effective. In fact one can imagine people like Blashford-Snell – 'Not Outer Mongolia again!' – finding a quiet evening by the fire a memorable 'event'. Combined with an opportunity to do good, especially as 'noble causes' can be rare on the shop floor or in many offices, Blood Donor Sessions like those organised by the Prudential Assurance company's 'Lifeline' can be an event.

Outside working hours, company related sporting events and charity challenges can promote team spirit and improve morale.

In fact in an action starved workplace virtually anything can be an event, but now some companies like Royal Mail have made events such an integral part of the motivation programme as to make them a way of life.

THE ROYAL MAIL 'THREE HUNDRED AND SIXTY FIVE DAY EVENT'

Bill Cockburn, the Managing Director of Royal Mail, began working for the Post Office when he left school 30 years ago and his long-term objective is to make it a World Class organisation – 'a benchmark that other people from around the world will come to see.'

'Our organisation was based on strong, centralised management and systems that were founded on the belief that our front-line employees were not to be trusted.

'What we are doing today is to dismantle all that and to trust our front-line employees. They have so much potential and the trick now is to liberate this and that means getting the training right, the communication right and the incentives and rewards right.

'We have set ourselves a number of "heroic goals" with the aim of driving out failure which is more expensive than success.'

They are goals which Royal Mail sought to achieve by a series of events involving all of the 180,000 people who operate the organisation for 365 days each year.

THE BACKGROUND TO GREAT EVENTS

Ian Raisbeck – a physicist by training – who was responsible for formulating and implementing 'Total Quality' for Rank Xerox International, is now Director of Quality for Royal Mail. He explained that in 1988 the company put together an overall directive for the organisation, one of the key elements of which was 'people working together to improve what they do'.

With this in mind, Royal Mail began to initiate 'PostCode Partnership Teams' to provide 'an opportunity to develop a local version of teamworking, involving managers in its development and creating local ownership.'

In other words the motivation effort was to be structured and managed. Teamworking would provide employees with motivating benefits including:

- a sense of belonging
- an understanding of team purpose
- support from within the team
- consistent and caring leadership
- involvement
- an opportunity to influence.

It was stressed that 'functional splits and settled attendances, while pre-requisites, would not deliver team working and that teamwork was not a stand alone concept.' The key requirements for effective teamworking were that teams should have:

- the same people, the same work processes and the same attendance time
- a recognised leader who is also a team member
- agreed common targets and goals – as part of an agreed customer supplier partnership
- displayed and updated performance measures
- process to aid the harmony of the group
- recognition
- team capability matching tasks

THE BENEFITS OF TEAMWORKING

Benefits to the customer would include increased expertise and reliability, plus a more personalised service allied to accountability.

The team members would benefit by building up team spirit and a sense of belonging. Their job expertise would be increased and they would enjoy more interesting jobs with more job satisfaction. They would be given the opportunity to influence, while teamworking would facilitate the recognition of their achievement and enable a better planning of their personal development. A note to the effect that teamworking could often result in better take-home pay, pensions, attendance patterns and annual leave opportunities than previous arrangements, meant that the whole of Maslow's Pyramid had been catered for.

As well as benefiting from increased customer confidence Royal Mail would create a more motivated, committed and purposeful workforce and improve its business performance.

THE TEAMWORK EVENT

Thus far, with in-house adaptations to cope with its size and the nature of its business, the Royal Mail Teamworking plan followed a laudable, well defined plan which had already proved effective, but it was at this stage that the whole thing took off and developed a life of its own by becoming an EVENT.

Said Ian Raisbeck, who was in charge of the latest teamwork event, 'We have people define what they do – and improve it. This is the very simple initial approach and, after beginning teamworking in 1989, we had the first teamwork event in 1990 when people came together to describe what they had done, working in teams, to improve certain aspects of their work. That was the first event which involved some 50 teams.

TOWARDS A GREAT EVENT

'The second national event in 1991 involved more than 100 teams but, more importantly, it had been fed into by 50 local events, some of which were beginning to approach in size the first event of 1990.'

We talked to Ian at the third annual teamwork event. It lasted two days during which 100 districts from around the country presented their best improvement project in the exhibition atmosphere of an enormous marquee in the grounds of the company's Milton Keynes training centre. Each of the 100 booths was manned by employees from the district concerned, who presented their projects and discussed them with visitors. Customers and external suppliers, such as Kodak and The Body Shop, also participated in the event.

Stand titles included 'Computerised Walk Testing' and a promise by one division 'to delight every customer with the most satisfying products in the most thought provoking shops ever – and to have fun and change the world for the better while we are at it.' (A neat summary of motivation in action.)

Stand titles like 'Communication for hard of hearing employees' and 'Royal Mail Contribution to the Paralympics' showed that 'noble causes' had not been forgotten.

THE EVENT AS AN IDEAS SHOP

In addition to outside visitors, more than 10,000 Royal Mail employees from all over Britain visited the event to find out for themselves what projects were being actioned and to select any they could use in their own areas of operation.

Managers and staff from all areas were able to brainstorm ideas in an enjoyable atmosphere and build up what amounted to an inventory of best practice. To make sure nothing was forgotten, all those attending the show were de-briefed on their homeward bound coaches to find out if there was a case for 'creative swiping'.

AN EVENT FOR THE FRONT LINE

Managing Director Bill Cockburn, who was at the 1992 EVENT – and visited every stand – stressed, 'A huge number of people here are front-line employees. We have empowered them and encouraged them to look into their experience and improve what they do; this is the key to success. All this drive for excellence at shop-floor level is marvellous. We are really giving people the opportunity to influence their working lives and we will be the richer for it, so what this event is all about is celebration, recognition of success and moving forward positively.'

A RECOGNITION EVENT

Ian Raisbeck stressed that the EVENT was the most effective form of recognition anyone could have. 'What you have here is people

LEADERSHIP: THE ART OF MOTIVATION

describing how they have worked together in a structured way using the basic processes and tools to achieve improvements.

'They are sharing good practice with all their colleagues and visitors and as a team they are able to show people and talk to people about what they have achieved.'

THE BOTTOM LINE

By now people throughout Royal Mail are striving to find an improvement important enough to get their teams through to the great EVENT, with quantifiable results throughout the organisation, as well as the non-quantifiable contribution in terms of things like morale.

Said Ian, 'There's one example from Hoddesdon where there has been a lot of new building going on.

'New buildings and new estates are hell for postmen as they are faced with unfamiliar walks, duplicated road names, roads split into two and so on, not to mention a whole population of "strangers to the district".

'In Hoddesdon a team has come up with a way of reducing mis-sorts and mis-deliveries dramatically.'

Another team devised a way of simplifying postmen's walk reviews, which once had to be recorded on a clip-board and transcribed back at the office – a process which took around four hours. Now, thanks to the team's work, postmen can record the required data automatically, and download it in about ten seconds.

. . . AND THE MILLION POUND TEAM

A Birmingham team, which included people using a sorting machine and the engineers who serviced it, looked into the question of increasing its output. Over a period of nine months they worked together to reprogramme the machine to handle 24 sorting bins instead of 12, and to do so more finely, which saves subsequent sorting work.

'What we have here', said Ian, 'is people looking at what we regard as a second generation of fairly old equipment and not only extending its useful life but extending its useful life at a capability level far beyond anything of which it was considered capable.'

The cost per sorting bin was £100 and, in addition to saving the cost of buying new machinery, the additional capability has resulted in a saving of £1m a year.

'It is quite dramatic,' agreed Ian, 'but in fact there were four or five very good examples from the Birmingham local EVENT. I was one of the group that had to make the selection of the one that would go forward to the National EVENT, and it wasn't easy. The million pound machine improvement team only won by a whisker from one or two of the others, so what you see at the National EVENT is only the tip of the iceberg.'

SUMMARY

- Some jobs are so dull and repetitive employees should get boredom pay. These jobs should be automated or filled by people who enjoy 'switching off'.
- Most jobs are routine at times. Liven up and motivate workers by supplying EVENTS, e.g. a Motivation Campaign.
- How Toyota (GB) turned what is usually a Sales and Marketing wing-ding for company top brass and customers into a motivating EVENT for all their staff.
- How the Royal Mail demonstrate the success of a classic motivation strategy by holding an EVENT which in three years has become a GREAT EVENT.

ACTION

- Check your business diary for the coming month for EVENTS including business lunches, interesting meetings, business trips, presentations, in fact anything that prevents YOUR job from becoming a matter of routine.
- Now imagine you are making a similar check on the diary of one of your shop-floor or office workers.
- Decide if an EVENT could be one way to motivate your people and if so what sort of EVENTS might be appropriate.

18. Motivating with Words

Words are one of the most powerful motivating forces there is and the manager who learns to use them effectively in all circumstances has the Field Marshal's baton of the business world in his grasp.

Unfortunately, communication between managers and their employees, and for that matter managers and other managers, is not always simple, largely because of the illusion that we all speak the same language. Today's managers have more sophisticated means of keeping in touch with their people and their colleagues than ever before, but this doesn't necessarily make things easier. In fact it often compounds the difficulties.

BASIC INTERNAL PUBLIC RELATIONS

There's an old Danish saying which advises: 'If you have no money – be polite', which reflects rather sadly on the way in which money and authority tend to erode people's manners.

Perhaps if it were rephrased to read: 'If you don't want to spend money – be polite', it would indicate the power of simple words like 'Please', 'Thank you', 'I wonder if you could help me', and 'Would you mind?' – motivating words which can all be used both when talking to individuals and when motivating a workforce.

Unfortunately some managers leave their good manners at their office door, while others are unfailingly well-mannered when talking to individuals, whatever their place in the organisation, but forget their manners entirely when addressing groups of employees or even the whole workforce. All of them could be spending time and money on incentives to persuade employees to do as they wish, when all they need do is ask – correctly.

MOTIVATING BY ASKING

In his famous article 'How do you motivate employees?' Frederick Herzberg answered his own question by asserting that the simplest, surest and most direct way of getting someone to do something was – to ask.

Unfortunately he didn't develop this theme and instead went on to say what he thought managers should do if the person in question refused, but his original advice is still valid; the best way to get one person or 100,000 people to do what you want to do is to ask them to do it.

In the workplace it is even easier for the manager to do this, as he has already got the authority to ask employees to do things, and there is an unspoken contract that in consideration for being paid they will – within limits – do as the manager asks.

However, if a manager asks incorrectly, he or she will provoke an 'equal and opposite re-action' and the requests will be complied with slowly and reluctantly, if at all.

Asking people to do things is an art, but fortunately it is one which most people possess in some measure so they need only polish and perfect it.

HOW TO ASK

American multi-millionaire Percy Ross has spent the last 20 years giving away money – to people who asked him for it in the right way. In his book '*Ask For the Moon and get it*' – a guide to how to ask correctly – he gives ten rules of asking, most of which can be adapted to the managerial situation. These include:

- Be certain of what you want to ask people to do. This sounds obvious but in fact many people are so anxious to avoid making a direct request that they shilly-shally until they have forgotten what it was they wanted in the first place. Write down the main headings of your request, especially if you are asking for something on the phone.

- Ask the right people and make sure that you get the name right. For instance if you are asking someone to do something for you by phone, and only know their position, check their name with the switchboard or with their secretary before they put you through.

- Prepare a good case. Once again, write down the main headings – post cards are very useful for this – so you can refer to them if need be; usually just knowing you have them available will be sufficient.

- Give if you want to receive. Make sure you know what's in it for 'them' – before 'they' ask.

- Don't be afraid to ask, and ask again; polite persistence pays.

- Ask with smiles, body language – yes, even on the phone – using tact, humour. Ask in such a way as to invite a 'yes'.

- Request and invite. Don't demand – even when you could – and don't beg.

- Show respect for the people you are asking to do things. This is immensely motivating. It's also extremely difficult to counterfeit, so managers who want to motivate their troops must get to know and appreciate them.

- Make asking a habit. Some managers use this ploy on colleagues as well as subordinates, working on the assumption that if they ask people to do simple things for them like passing papers or relaying messages they develop the habit of obedience. If done consciously this smacks of manipulation rather than motivation.

- Introduce 'us' and 'we' when asking people to do things.

- An additional rule of asking – and one of the great secrets of leadership – is to be absolutely certain that people will do as you ask. The art of this sort of assumption, which usually takes on the force of a self-fulfilling prophecy, lies in making it clear that it is not them but their compliance which you are taking for granted.

To ask in the ways outlined above we need to be able to communicate and that means that people must be able to understand us. As far as we know there are no figures on the amount of managerial 'bumf' thrown away unread because the people it was intended to motivate couldn't understand it, but it must make a nasty hole in the rain forest.

KEEP IT SIMPLE

Managerial jargon can be a useful shorthand for communication between managers; it can also be a recognition signal, an elitist language and an opportunity to demonstrate 'superior' education.

It often goes hand in hand with sesquipedalianism, a splendidly appropriate word for a tendency to use long words.

Unfortunately both jargon and sesquipedalianism can be contagious and most people exposed to them for any length of time will find themselves 'commencing', 'prioritising' and 'facilitating' with the best.

They are not a good way of getting over a motivating message to your workforce as – in addition to making it difficult to understand what you mean – they reinforce the de-motivating 'them' and 'us' conditioning which you should be trying to get rid of.

CHOOSING THE MOTIVATING WORDS

Choosing the most motivating words and the most motivating way in which to put them across is not easy but asking the Five W questions will usually help.

- WHO? A bunch of bishops or a meeting of miners? Your language could be different for each group, but unless you are a cleric or a miner you should not try to imitate the speech of either, merely shade your own language in the direction of theirs. A useful tip is to think of the people you wish to motivate in terms of the newspapers they read. For example, if you are communicating with large numbers of people – think tabloid. Mass circulation newspapers – which often put over complicated ideas as well as simple ones – use language all their readers will understand and feel comfortable with.

- WHAT? Decide what it is that you wish to motivate people to do. The message should dictate your language and vocabulary whatever medium you use. Short sharp Anglo-Saxon words toughen up your message. Softer words of French origin can be more conciliatory.

- WHEN? When things are going badly the need for motivating words is obvious, but it is easy enough to forget the need for motivating words of congratulation once your people have dug you out of the mire. Say 'Thank you'. For one thing it's good manners and for another you will almost certainly need their help again.

- WHERE? You will usually be motivating your people in the workplace. This lends your words useful extra authority. It also means that any facile assurances you may make could be regarded as firm promises.

In the end your internal Public Relations effort should result in a change in the culture/conditioning of the WHO? which will make it a great deal easier for you to ask them to do things.

HOW? THE TOOLS OF INTERNAL PUBLIC RELATIONS

- Notice-boards
- Posters
- Letters
- Newsletters
- Leaflets
- Brochures
- House Journals
- Special employee reports i.e. annual pension fund reports
- Videos
- Computer-on screen-newspaper. Electronic mail.

- Briefing groups, conferences and seminars

NOTICE-BOARDS

Notice-boards are a good way of expressing public recognition of individual or group achievements. They are usually associated with prosaic managerial announcements but managers can sometimes make use of this sober image by introducing a 'shock' element of humour. For example there was the national newspaper editor who used the newsroom notice-board to motivate better writing by announcing that 'In future reporters who write for this newspaper will avoid cliches like the plague.' There is a good case for two distinct types of notice-board, one for official bulletins, and one for employees' small ads, social announcements and so on.

POSTERS

These can be excellent motivators if properly used. However, even the best have a short shelf life and all posters should be replaced before they reach their die-by date, if need be by a different poster expressing the same message.

Humour can often be used effectively, and one example of good practice in this respect comes from the Prudential Assurance Company Life Administrations offices in Reading who wanted to motivate staff to update their internal telephone directory. They used a series of black and white posters with strong effective cartoons, in one of which for example a fire and brimstone parson thundered 'Are you a directory sinner? Do you have a new extension and the directory has your old extension? If yes, you are a sinner. Contact RLS/Telecoms on exts . . . and may they have mercy on your soul.' Others implied that girls who had 'gone crazy for Swayze' and boys who were 'a gonna for Madonna', and were still waiting for a call from their idols, had only themselves to blame if their extension numbers were out of date.

LETTERS

A good way of 'personalising' motivating messages. Like all other business letters, letters to employees should be: clear, short – one page for preference – and deal with ONE main topic only. Small margins and cramped signatures look 'mean'. Use a style only fractionally more formal than normal conversation.

- Wrong – 'Smith B. The current economic recession means that all employees of Brown and Co. are going to have to work a lot harder and with this in mind we have instituted the following procedures. Failure to comply will be dealt with severely . . .'
- Better – 'Dear Barbara Smith. Largely because of the state of the economy, in spite of everyone's efforts, we at Brown and Co. have not been doing as well as we need to do. However, there are some positive moves we can make to increase our efficiency, several of which have been suggested by members of staff . . .'

NEWSLETTERS

These fall into two broad categories.:

1. 'Service' newsletters which are usually written by and for employees but funded by employers as part of the social benefits packages for their staff. Large employers like banks and insurance companies often produce this type of magazine in which – though they may contain some company or product news – staff news, gossip and articles predominate. A good example of this type is *Progress*, a four-page yellow coloured news sheet produced by a team from Royal Mail, Great Yarmouth, as 'Frontline News'. Unashamedly a home-grown product, the 'yellow peril' provides news and tips, news from Teamwork Groups, sports and social news.
2. 'Motivational' newsletters. These are written by or on behalf of management with the aim of informing and motivating staff.

Typical corporate users of this kind of newsletter are large hotel chains who want to create a family atmosphere among groups of employees spread across a large number of locations. Motivating newsletters should:

- highlight success
- focus on people
- present changes in company working practices etc. in a positive light
- encourage response from readers

Newsletters of this sort need punchy headlines, tightly written, easy to read copy, good quality photographs and a high standard of design etc. Stories about the company and its promotions should be balanced by stories about the staff, including 'gossip'.

Offering prizes for story leads, workplace tips and so on helps create the feeling of 'ownership'. Lengthy first-person comments from senior management do the opposite.

THE PROFESSIONAL TOUCH

Motivational newsletters are usually professionally produced by editorial staff from the firm's PR department or consultancy. *In Touch*, for example, a newsletter produced by Saatchi and Saatchi's Bristol based Hall Harrison Cowley Agency for Country Club Hotels, is slick, well designed and announces major company news, like the start of the move into Europe, on the front page. Inside, there's a feature on training and a training round up, plus briefs on company news – like new golf courses and kitchens – and the announcement of an incentive scheme for 'super service', plus an 'editionalised' back page of local company news like the 'Congratulations' item on the kitchen porter named as Forest of Arden's Employee of the Year.

Leaflets and Brochures

These are fine for introducing campaigns or special events. They are a relatively costly way of getting information to a captive audience but can provide a useful means of obtaining instant feed-back by means of response forms.

House Journals

Professionally produced newspapers and magazines, often of high standard both in design and content. *Railnews* for example, the newspaper of British Rail, is a 44-page tabloid distributed free to every BR employee in the first week of every month.

Well written and interestingly presented, it provides an ideal vehicle for management motivation exercises, together with stories demonstrating what a huge and on the whole successful undertaking the railways are, plus grass roots contributions including a page for employee 'grouses'. A quick column-inch advertisement count indicates it may also be self-funding or better.

The arrival of a journal of this sort, especially if one's name is in it, is an EVENT.

Videos

Videos can be used in an internal Public relations role as well as in a training role and BR for example, as well as commissioning a video explaining how to set up Quality Improvement teams, also had one made featuring its Quality Fair 1991 at the NEC Birmingham. Copies were sent to all 214 teams who had stands at the Fair and distributed up and down the railway 'so those who couldn't come could see what all the fuss was about.'

UNIPART GO ONE BETTER – WELL, A FEW MILLION BETTER REALLY

When Unipart put on the Epcot theatrical show in Warwick to introduce their new image they had a video made which is still being used to motivate staff.

In addition, the company now has a monthly company video called *Grapevine* with regular slots for company affairs, social news and a licence to use critical or self-critical material. For instance one edition featured a Senior Manager admitting he had been wrong to insist for so long on the adoption of an expensive Japanese solution to a particular problem and that, in the end, an idea put forward by an in-house ideas group had proved better and cheaper.

Playing the company video is an EVENT but Unipart now has not only an in-house video but an in-house video production team. Explained Chief Executive John Neil. 'In 1987 when we did the privatisation, we realised that to make it work we were going to have to do a huge amount of communications, using videos and so on.

'The costs in those days were horrific. TV commercials cost a thousand pounds a second. Video filming, largely because of trade union restrictive practices, cost a thousand pounds a minute. So we decided to make our own, bought a camera and hired one guy who knew how to use it. He kept asking for more people and they did work in-house and by 1990 they were so good that we set them up as an agency and they are now between 30 and 40 strong and turning over between £4.4m and £5m a year. They do a fair bit of external business now and have an independent Chairman.'

BRIEFING GROUPS, CONFERENCES AND SEMINARS

Briefings, conferences and seminars have an obvious motivating role. Professional one day management seminars are popular motivators. Once the prerogative of top and upper middle management, they have cascaded in many companies to junior management.

Seminars – the Latin root means seeding – are an ideal way of sowing a motivating message and usually include motivating elements of participation and socialising. The acid test of a really good seminar is whether delegates would have considered paying for it with their own money.

One recent practice in big companies is to train home-grown speakers to put the company message on motivation across to groups which eventually cover the whole of the work force. Occasions of this sort have the added motivation of an EVENT.

COMPUTERS AND IN-HOUSE PUBLIC RELATIONS

One of the latest motivating in-house Public Relations ideas in companies with computer linked offices, or computer operating employees who work from home, is a computer based newsletter which can be punched up on the employee's VDU – one of the many uses of electronic mail. The proportion of management content to employee contributions can be varied and the fact that management could scan at any time provides a measure of control without censorship. Material can be updated at will and management suggestions, for example, could provoke instant feedback, while both management and employee ideas could be electronically brainstormed without participants leaving their offices – or their homes.

PUBLIC RELATIONS EVENTS

Large organisations are able to run internal PR EVENTS like BR's 'Young Environmentalist of the Year Award' which is open to young people aged 8-16 who are relatives of company employees or pensioners.

These are motivating in the sense of adding to the 'company as a family' image. However they would be something of a luxury for smaller organisations who can get the same effect by supporting employee charity efforts.

THE MAN WITH THE GOLDEN VAN – A PUBLIC RELATIONS BONUS

Public Relations, whether internal or external, home-grown or consultancy generated, are not often 'something for nothing'. They are usually the result of hard thinking on the part of some individual or group whose ideas and recommendations can seem so simple and obvious as to be pure common sense. The effects are often unquantifiable.

However, there are times when PR produces a bonus, as is the case with Royal Mail Parcel Force's 'Gold Depot Awards', the National Winners of which get the use of a special Golden Van for three months. This provides not only great motivating 'recognition' for the winners and good internal PR but a bonus of external PR every time the Golden Van takes to the streets.

Award panels, including customers, select six Best Depots on the basis of a number of 'Conditions of Excellence' including: exceptional customer service, innovation, customer comments and safe driving. In addition to a chance of becoming a Gold Depot and driving the Golden Van, area winners are presented with a cheque to give to the charity or good cause of their choice.

Successes like that of the Golden Van – which fundamentally cost little more than the paint – are not the only bonus internal PR can provide and the PR man's dream is a single idea which costs virtually nothing to implement, or is self-funded, but which takes off, once the original leaders have been motivated, to become an unstoppable wave of enthusiasm. Such ideas have created world religions, spread political systems and turned unknown singers into multi-millionaires. It's pleasant to think that the same motivating forces, if properly managed, could do the same for your business, if you or your people can come up with one world beating idea.

SUMMARY

- How to motivate people to do what you want by asking them correctly.

- The magic words of asking – good manners yet again.
- The rules of asking as laid down by a multi-millionaire philanthropist and how they can be adapted to the managerial situation.
- How internal Public Relations can improve your chances of success by changing the climate in which you ask your people to do what you want and eventually affecting their conditioning.
- The tools of motivation PR and how to use them. How one firm turned one aspect of its internal PR effort into an independent company worth millions of pounds.

ACTION

- Check your organisation's internal PR. Who is responsible? Has it been neglected in favour of external PR?
- Ask yourself if you could rely on every one of your employees to do half an hour's unpaid overtime – or an hour's paid overtime – in an emergency. If you couldn't, your internal PR needs an overhaul.
- Check which PR tools you are already using to motivate your people. Could you use more or make a different approach? Don't forget to listen: the best internal PR ideas often come from the people concerned. Accentuate the 'relations' in your Public Relations.
- Try to think of the 'big' motivating PR idea. Today could be the day you leap out of the tub shouting 'Eureka!'

19. Choosing a Motivating Style

Deciding how you motivate will depend on who you want to motivate and what you want to motivate them to do, but in the end it is you who will have to decide on a motivating style which is not only appropriate to your employees but which suits you.

If you are the intellectual type, never happier than when working on flow charts and organisational diagrams, then the flamboyant, show biz style approach to motivation may not be for you.

On the other hand, if you are a hail-fellow-well-met manager who directs successful operations with one hand firmly round a pint pot, the type of motivation campaign which requires a 1,000 page handbook with daily supplements might not suit you.

Mind you, in many cases you will be aiming to alter your employees' culture and the shock of a complete change of personality would certainly grab their attention.

In fact there are enough styles to choose from and the best of them are a mix with a personal emphasis rather than a totally one-sided approach.

HORSES FOR COURSES

Here are a few examples of best practice, some of them idiosyncratic to the point of eccentricity, others experimenting with what may be the motivation style of the twenty-first century and still others building carefully on the known.

They have two things in common:

1. Wherever they place the emphasis, none of the main motivating factors is neglected.
2. They have all been extremely successful.

BANISHING GRIPES

Some motivation methods are a little difficult to emulate unless, like British Gas, you have 17 million or so customers. As Robert Evans, Chairman and Chief Executive, told us, 'When British Gas was privatised in 1986 it was important to instil a new sense of customer service and to make all employees, but particularly those working at the "sharp end", take greater pride in providing what the customer wanted. So motivation of staff was a key factor in improving customer service.'

The motivation effort began with the launch of a 'Banish Gripes' media campaign to let customers, shareholders and staff know that British Gas aimed to do 'even better in every way.'

A questionnaire was sent out to all 17 million domestic customers asking them how they rated certain aspects of British Gas service. One and a quarter million replies were received and the results used to identify areas where the company could make improvements.

Said Robert Evans, 'I wrote to all members of staff enclosing the questionnaire before it was sent to customers, so there was employee involvement from the outset.'

The survey indicated a need for higher standards of service and within three months a practical guide – *A Commitment to Our Customer* – was published which laid down the standards and quality of service customers could expect in showrooms, on the phone and when having appliances repaired.

'It let our customers know what to expect but also ensured that every person who worked for British Gas knew what was expected of them.' The Citizens' Charter meant some changes to the *Commitment to Customers* guidelines, and British Gas took the opportunity to implement a new motivation initiative by telling managers how to involve and motivate their staff.

The results? In the latest MORI survey 85 per cent of customers expressed themselves as satisfied with the service British Gas provides. 'This could not have been achieved without the efforts of a motivated workforce with a strong sense of self-worth' asserted Robert Evans.

THE RICHER WAY

Richer Sounds have 15 retail shops in 11 cities throughout the United Kingdom and their aim is to have a shop in every town or city with a population of more than 200,000.

The company was founded in 1978 by its Chairman Julian Richer who owns 100 per cent of it and is a charismatic, slightly eccentric leader who genuinely believes that motivating staff is the only way to get them to provide good customer service.

At first sight his approach to motivation seems brash, but it is in fact tailor-made for his youthful team in which the average age of the managers is 24 and most of the Directors are only about two years older.

AIMS AND OBJECTIVES

Julian is totally clear about the aims and objectives of his company – which last year made a profit of £1 million on £16 million turnover – and how he motivates to achieve them.

He defines these aims in his company's philosophy 'The Richer Way':

1. To provide second to none service and value for our customers
2. To provide ourselves with secure, well paid jobs, working in a stimulating equal opportunities environment
3. To be profitable and to ensure our long term growth and survival

In this short statement of aims Richer Sounds has already

announced 'a noble cause', proclaimed its intention of providing for a whole raft of 'needs', and has made a dent in 'them' and 'us', while introducing a re-assuring note of enlightened self-interest.

Julian Richer adds more to his motivation package with factors like:

- Stimulation. He maintains that work must be fun and is always looking for new ways to 'keep the buzz going'.
- Appreciation and recognition.
- Good rewards and job security.

The Package

Sales assistants outside London regularly earn more than £15,000 a year, while warehouse assistants earn an average of £12,000 plus overtime and profit sharing.

Managers are entitled to an XR 3i car or the cash equivalent, while Regional Directors get a Porsche or equivalent which comes equipped with car phone.

All employees, who are known as 'colleagues', receive a profit share depending on the level of their seniority in the company.

The Motivating Machine

When they join the firm and pick up their 'Welcome' pack, giving everything from the history of the company to health advice, new 'colleagues' join a motivating machine in which nothing seems to have been forgotten.

For example, the London HQ is decorated from floor to ceiling with customers' letters of appreciation, while the shops, though cramped, have a good atmosphere and staff are encouraged to put up amusing signs and photographs. In addition each shop is provided with a fridge and a microwave for the use of colleagues.

Along with the welcome pack comes a Training Manual to help with the three days training all recruits have to undergo before jettisoning their training badges. In addition, each sales assistant has an appointed 'shadow' to help them in their early days with the company, a motivating gesture which anyone who has ever been a new boy – or girl – will appreciate.

THE FIRM THAT REALLY DOES – SEND THE ROLLS

New colleagues could also be surprised to learn that, as winners in the 'Richer Way League', members of the best performing branch or department share the use of a Rolls Royce for a month.

Shops are judged on response to customer service questionnaires, performance, and procedures, and winners also have their names engraved on a brass plate in Julian's office.

To help motivate good service in this way each customer is given a receipt which includes a questionnaire asking about the sales assistant's performance. For each 'excellent' ticked, the assistant is given £2 and if the customer writes in to say how good the service was, they are given £4.

Other motivating benefits include the fact that Julian Richer's country house in Yorkshire is available for holidays to all staff who have served more than five years with the company.

There is free life insurance, worth two years' salary, and 75 per cent subsidised PPP membership for all staff, plus free medical advice from top consultants for employees not satisfied with that of their own GP. Interest free loans are available in case of hardship and there is a Welfare Fund of one per cent of profits for colleagues' use in case of crisis.

There are also gold aeroplanes for high fliers, together with dinners with the boss and gifts for long service.

AND THE INTANGIBLES

All promotion is from within the company and staff are promoted on ability 'irrespective of age, colour, sex, background, education or time with the company.'

All sales assistants, managers and regional directors attend twice yearly training seminars at Julian Richer's house, in addition to which there are weekly educational talks for sales assistants by the Technical Service Manager. Not surprisingly, staff turnover is 'practically zero', and in a 1990 survey 96 per cent of staff said it was 'fun' to work for Richer Sounds whose motivation policies have enabled them to claim the largest sales per square foot retail operation in the world, with the most successful staff suggestion scheme in the UK currently running at 1,500 suggestions a year – an average of 20 per employee – possibly because every suggestion is read by the boss who awards tax free cash or exotic trips to winners.

THE CASE OF THE HEADLESS BODY SHOP

The Body Shop began in Brighton in 1976 when Anita Roddick opened a shop to sell naturally based skin and hair preparations which were simply packaged and in a convenient range of sizes. The contrast with the overpackaged, overpriced products of her rivals was almost enough on its own to ensure her success and The Body Shop took off – world wide.

TEAMWORKING WITHOUT MANAGERS

In late 1991, when opening its latest branch in London's West End, the company decided it wanted a shop which would provide 'the ultimate in customer service.'

The Directors – who in the days before motivation language would have called in eight people and told them what they wanted – 'briefed an eight strong Task Force', including the Human Resources Manager, a General Manager, an Area Manager, the Training Manager and the Field Training Manager. After brainstorming a number of ideas they came up with the project of a managerless group of people, working as a team.

RECRUITMENT BECOMES CASTING

Realising that a chance to 'hire the best' was an opportunity to control the WHO?, The Body Shop – using the theatrical 'A Star is

Born' theme throughout – designed an audition-style assessment for people who replied to their advertisement asking for 'performers'. This tested the applicant's ability to smile a lot, their interpersonal skills, teamplay, creativity, initiative, confidence level, approachability and positive attitude.

Said Jane Corson, The Body Shop's Human Resources Manager, 'We decided that too often time is spent concentrating on previous job experience rather than on personality.'

The best people from the audition were then put through a further assessment day lasting about eight hours, to provide an indication of possible 'management' skills i.e. leadership, initiative and organisation. In between the audition and assessment candidates had to prepare a C.V. and write an essay on 'Customer Care'.

INVOLVE TO SOLVE

The Body Shop hoped that more involvement by all staff would lead to higher levels of motivation and morale with 'more of a buzz in the atmosphere'. The team, chosen partly by staff from other stores, trained together for four weeks, after which members were asked to allocate themselves to four sub-groups: financial, stock, shopfloor, human resources/training. In addition to operational training, team members were also taught decision making and communication skills.

Team members, or 'performers', chose their own jobs on the basis of who wanted to do what and who had the appropriate skills. On a day to day basis it was they who decided on the volume of stock, training and shift patterns, although the overall responsibility was that of the Area Manager who would carry the can if something went badly wrong at the Oxford Street store.

TEAMWORKING

The experiment was to be the ultimate in teamworking and the company patiently selected people who would be motivated by self-actualisation and then, after formal training, empowered them to a great degree with the aim of identifying new style managers with the participative, team building, team leading style they see as the way forward.

THE CRITICS REVIEW

Teams review each other's performance on forms headed 'The Body Shop Critics Review', giving Thumbs Up, Thumbs Down or Rave reviews to items like Sales Satisfaction, Appearance, Teamwork, Flexibility, Time Keeping, Communication, Speed of Work and Initiative.

Copies of the reviews are sent to Head Office and the occasional 'mystery customer' checks to see that all is well. Otherwise – apart from knowing that help is available should it be needed – the performers, who like all The Body Shop employees are in the company's profit sharing scheme, are very much on their own.

The indications are that the performers have been motivated by the 'spice' of running their own show to become more involved in the working of the store as a whole and to take pride in their jobs. It also seems as though some of the performers are on the way to becoming stars who will no doubt be given more important roles in the future. Because of this secondary aim of the experiment, the time element at the team formation phase was of less importance than it might otherwise have been. Note that, once the motivation had been generated by the teams, elements of structure and management – i.e. controls and reports – were in place.

WHEN EAST MEETS WEST

Treating shop floor staff as managers by putting them in control of their own work has also been the approach to motivation at Yamazaki Machinery Worcester, the £65 million turnover subsidiary of the world's largest producer of computer controlled machine tools.

Explained Total Quality Control Manager, Doctor Akimasa Kurimoto, 'Instead of paying ten "inspectors" to do the inspection, our shop floor employees inspect every stage of the manufacturing process and to do this we have had to bring up the standards of all our 220 shop floor people to inspector level.'

Yamazaki are dedicated to continuous improvement and regard training as a long-term investment. For example, all new recruits attend a week long induction course conducted by senior managers and directors on the corporate business strategy, advanced manufacturing concepts and total quality management philosophy.

The company emphasises participation among employees at all levels and tries to avoid the traditional 'top-down' approach. This means that staff at all levels are regarded as vital to the organisation, there is mutual respect and everyone contributes to obtain mutual benefits. Significantly, everyone regards the shop floor as the core of the business and managers make certain of this by involving the shop floor in any local decisions that are taken in the light of in-depth knowledge. The management's responsibility is to provide the correct climate in which the workforce can create a better working atmosphere.

RECOGNITION

After four years of operation, the Worcester plant – completed in 1987 – was awarded one of only ten 'Best in the World' ratings by the Royal Swedish Academy of Engineering Sciences, who said Yamazaki's success was due to the way in which people were trained and motivated. The company had fulfilled for its employees 'the three fundamental human needs: to belong to a group and feel a sense of solidarity; to have work assignments that feel meaningful; to be able to influence one's own situation.'

At the time the company was operating a temporary bonus scheme which depended strictly on the achievement of clearly defined production targets i.e. a specific number of machines. The assessors wondered what would happen when the scheme ended.

'In fact,' says Dr. Kurimoto, 'we no longer operate a bonus scheme and morale is extremely high. Absenteeism for instance is very low – averaging one point five per cent, partly because we emphasise mutual trust between the management and shop floor and give workers a large degree of autonomy and partly because employees don't wish to let down the other members of their team.'

Paying for Potential

Yamazaki don't neglect the financial incentive but their approach is unusual and effective.

Using a comprehensive personal development appraisal formula, the degree of 'technical knowledge, multi-skills, responsibility, conformity and leadership' are fully appraised by the employee's immediate superior and discussed in detail with the individual concerned every 12 months. Based on this appraisal employees can set their own personal targets for the next six months or year and the company will give them every possible help in achieving them.

Said Dr Kurimoto, 'Pay is based not only on people's performance and their attitude to their work but also on their potential.'

The 'Thinking' Culture

'The important thing,' Doctor Kurimoto stressed, 'is to develop a thinking culture. Management can come up with ideas but the right way is for each operative to think of the best way to do things.

'This year we have 55 teams and each team studies, on average, three subjects, which means that we get 165 items to be improved. In the last five years some 800 subjects have been improved – a tremendous overall achievement'.

The thinking culture meant for instance that, because flexibility and multi-skilling had already been introduced for everyone, the shop floor did not adopt the traditional negative attitudes to the introduction of robot welding but, after discovering that robot welding was three times as productive as manual welding, actually welcomed the new technology as something which would make their lives easier.

USING RECESSION TO MOTIVATE

One part of Yamazaki policy their employees must find extremely motivating is the company's attitude towards recession and redundancy. Said Dr Kurimoto, 'During recession time most companies make redundancies simply because it's the cheapest and quickest way to resolve their cash flow problem.

'By contrast, we want to retain our skilled workforce – it takes about three years for them to attain the required level of technical skill – so we have used recession time to intensify the training of our staff who are encouraged to seek training in the use of more sophisticated machinery. Yamazaki also use the recession time, when we have some spare capacity, to launch brand new models. In this way we can sort out the problems and be ready, when the recession ends, to produce more of the new models which is extremely competitive.'

TOGETHER-SUCCESS

'Together-Success' is the motto of the organisation whose U.K. operation has achieved a high degree of motivation by treating its workforce as skilled adults who are encouraged and helped to attain their full potential – which benefits both the individual and the company.

THE SELF-PROPELLED PROPELLOR MAKERS

Kam-e-wa, who are a part of the Vickers Marine Engineering group, are the world's number one manufacturers of marine propellors.

At their Swedish factory the 500 workers are divided into flow groups of 20 employees, so autonomous that each group virtually runs its own business or profit centre. The groups have their own managers and are responsible not only for production but for personnel, purchasing, costing and dealing with other groups as internal customers.

As a result production has increased enormously, absenteeism is almost non-existent and people are behaving as though they were self-employed. Once again the policy of involving employees by empowering them to make important decisions has paid dividends in terms of motivation and morale, but what happens if decisions have to be made which could cost millions?

MOTIVATING THE MILLION POUND MANAGERS

Texaco's solution to the problems posed by marginal North Sea fields has made them pioneers in sub-sea technology. It has also persuaded them to locate their drilling and production departments in Aberdeen, which has brought decision-making closer to the front line.

The Strathspey team, for instance, was set up in 1990 with the specific goal of engineering and building the facilities to produce gas and oil from the Strathspey Field, one of the largest of the North Sea oil fields to be developed with sub-sea technology. At £398 million, it is also one of the most expensive and complex sub-sea developments ever attempted by the company. A fully integrated and multi-disciplinary team achieved the requisite flexible structure; it included geologists, engineers, and construction and commercial personnel who pooled all their expertise together rather than having everyone work from their own separate divisions in a vertical structure. Texaco further developed a functional organisation by reducing the layers of management from nine to three, with higher levels of delegation and increased individual responsibility.

PASSING ON THE MOTIVATION

The Strathspey team passed on the 'empowerment' motivation to their contractors by encouraging them to take the initiative in putting forward new and specific proposals, rather than merely asking them for their standard solutions – a strategy which resulted in a 10 per cent saving on estimates. Texaco realise that freedom and decision-making power go hand in hand with the possibility of mistakes, but this is a risk that has generally paid off for the company.

MEANWHILE – BACK AT THE OFFICE

Motivating shop assistants whose work can be judged on financial results and the way they interact with customers, or high powered oil company managers whose lives are filled with risk and interest, is one thing – but how do you motivate people who work in, say, the administrative offices of an insurance company?

Dr Steve Tanner, who has a degree in chemistry and a DPhil in enzymology, worked for Ford and ICL before joining the Prudential's Life Administration Unit in Reading two years ago as Quality Initiative Manager.

His problem was that, after putting a great deal of time and effort into designing new procedures, people 'hadn't even got the motivation to read the procedures so they weren't following them.'

Says Steve, 'We were relying on their understanding that when we invest in improvement action it is to their benefit as well as the company's, but we hadn't actually got the involvement we would have liked.'

FINDING A GOAL

Steve's solution was to set people an unusual goal. 'I decided we should go in for BS5750 and use motivation techniques to help us to get it. No one in insurance had BS5750 and I thought it would be a good thing if we were the first company to get it'.

The BS5750 is the standard of the British Standards Institute and is virtually the same as the international standard ISO9000. It is designed to provide a management framework in which to achieve quality. As Steve realised, it is a way of providing both a goal and a structure for an organisation's motivation effort.

The Employment Department explains that BS5750 is a

common sense approach which enables people to set down the following points on paper in an organised way:

- what they do
- the justification for what they do
- the evidence that they do what they say
- a record of what they did
- take action to improve what they do

Normally BS5750 is demanded by customers who announce that they will only do business with companies that have got it, which usually means that one person gets lumbered with all the paperwork entailed by submitting the report and that, in fact, very little changes.

Steve did not want this to happen and decided to make the rather boring BS5750 process into an event that would involve all the staff and lead to continuous improvement.

'Because the Industrial Branch Administration in Prudential as a unit would get no marketing benefit out of BS5750 I knew it would be purely self-medication and that it would only work if we got 100 per cent involved. I had to get people interested in what they were doing in order to achieve motivation, as a unit.

The aims were defined as: 'changing people's behaviour, invigorating the organisation, increasing customer focus, introducing a common language and involving everyone'; the performance aims were: 'to improve accuracy, speed and morale, to meet customer expectations and to reduce costs'.

PRODDING THE PRU

To help them achieve BS5750 Steve decided to appoint a motivation consultant, Robin Walker of IML: 'a difficult decision as there are some things that are not part of the Prudential culture.

'In practice it worked out amazingly well, because when we first briefed the teams on what they were to do and gave them background information on the project – i.e. to get BS5750 – they weren't interested, but when we said "Oh, and by the way, from Monday you are going to wear badges with 'FIVE-O-GO!' on them" the atmosphere changed and the barriers began to break down.

'We actually took people through the stages of the certification process of the BS5750 process and that's quite difficult, because you are motivating people for quite a length of time and motivating them to reach a milestone – and then to go further.

'In the end people were meeting in each others' homes to discuss BS5750 procedures – one area had a karaoke night and sang songs about quality.

'Some of the older people thought it was degrading but we got 90 per cent involvement and, when it came to doing BS5750, instead of it being led by management, which would have been the norm two or three years ago, it was fully accepted that people of junior grades were leading the teams.

'Now some of the people who were key players in the motivation plan have gained promotion.'

Mainly because Steve Tanner was able to stimulate the involvement of virtually all of the staff, BS5750 – which normally takes a year to obtain – was achieved in six months. They were six months in which the staff of Life Administration also managed to change their culture, so much so that managers now feel able, for example, to give recognition to file clerks who achieve the biggest reduction in out of date files – the equivalent at the hitherto overprudent Pru of 'sending the Rolls.'

COMPANY BENEFITS

The company has benefited from this revolution in its culture by a measurable increase in efficiency and accuracy, huge money savings and an appreciable improvement in staff morale.

The Prudential became the first insurance company to have part of its organisation awarded BS5750 registration and, following that, Life Administration won the 1991 Institute of Administrative Management Award for administrating Total Quality.

In addition, says Steve, 'we now manage our business a lot tighter and a lot better as a result of gaining registration.'

Steve's personal achievement has been recognised and he now lectures regularly at Department of Trade and Industry seminars on the benefits of BS5750 and the way the Prudential achieved it using motivation.

The Belfast office of Industrial Branch Administration won the Northern Ireland Quality Award for Service. 'The Award was granted for making rapid progress in achieving inspirational commitment from all managers and staff, so transforming an office working environment into a challenging and stimulating place to work', said the judges.

As for IML, who found the use of BS5750 to structure and direct the Pru's motivation effort so successful, they are now offering a 'FIVE-O-GO! Campaign as one of the company's major products.

SUMMARY

- The Richer Way or how to motivate with money, cars and country houses – while not forgetting appreciation.
- The case of the Headless Body Shop. How The Body Shop trains managers by eliminating management in its new Bond Street store.
- The Japanese Way – training shop floor workers to manage their machines and themselves.
- The self-propelled propellor makers of Sweden.
- Texaco – how to motivate top managers to create a successful sub-sea oilfield installation by giving them responsibility.
- Motivating karaoke sessions at the Prudential. How setting an important goal changed people's way of like in Life Administration and turned them into winners.

ACTION

- Identify the common motivating factors in these diverse motivating styles, i.e. incentives, challenge, involvement.
- Compare the flamboyant and the not so flamboyant with your current motivating style. Is there a case for a change of emphasis?

20. Motivation, Means and Opportunity

Most managers accept the need for motivation in an increasingly competitive world, but many still refuse to admit that there are people in all grades of their organisation who can be trained and developed to the benefit of both the individual and the company.

Richard Phillips, who lectures in leadership and teamwork at Ashridge Management College, begins by giving managers a questionnaire which asks them to rank motivating factors in order of their importance to themselves.

They are then asked to fill in the same questionnaire giving the order of importance in which they think the same factors would be placed by their people.

Richard says, 'I have a computer worksheet which does the numbers for me and almost invariably over the years the overall valuation indicates something like, "Well, I'm the manager and I'm motivated by lofty ideals like achievement and so on, whereas my people, being who they are, are only interested in money."

'This is the key confrontation. Many of the managers haven't been confronted with their mistaken assumptions before and that usually works quite powerfully to alert them to the fact that other people are probably pretty similar to themselves.'

The Lingering 'Them' and 'Us'

Sadly, many employees also feel that if they are hired for a position at the bottom of the organisational ladder that is almost certainly where they will end their working lives, and that the only way in which they can improve their lot is by fighting for more pay and better conditions. In organisations like this, motivation at shop-floor and general office level often means little more than creating enthusiasm and improving morale which – while a good beginning to any motivation effort – still leaves human resources untapped.

CHANGING THE CULTURE

Unfortunately, management's motivating initiatives frequently meet with scepticism from the workforce who, while happy enough to play motivating games which relieve boredom and raise morale, are less willing to take part in formal training schemes which some see as a potential betrayal of the 'us' in favour of the 'them'.

These days, the culture of most organisations is changing slowly, at least to a point where people can be motivated to take part in projects like Quality programmes, and there are indications that people are asking for more, and requesting the training which will enable them to assume the responsibility on offer.

MOTIVATE THEM YOUNG

Modern managers would find it difficult to set up infant schools as Robert Owen did, in order to 'grow their own' motivated workforce, but there is a case for companies involving themselves with local schools by perhaps providing equipment and personnel for combined charitable projects, or donating out of date but usable equipment for training purposes.

Managers should also make it plain that they consider the careers master to hold one of the most important posts in the school and that they are anxious to hire the best – even in hard times.

Some companies invite the families of new recruits, once confirmed in their jobs, to visit the workplace and see for themselves what the work is like and what the prospects are.

It is not enough to tell recruits or their families that 'They'll do all right if they work hard.' New members of the company have to know for certain that, as a matter of policy, the top positions in the organisation are achievable by all who want them enough to train and to work for them, and the machinery is in place to enable them to do this.

MOTIVATE THEM FIT

Many companies have now discovered that physical fitness is not only motivating in itself but, like sport, can provide challenges analogous to those employees will meet in the workplace.

Some – like IBM, TSB, Friendly Hotels and Unipart – have installed corporate health and fitness centres.

Unipart's professionally run health and fitness centre, the 'Lean Machine', for example, was opened at the group's Cowley HQ in 1992 to cater for everyone, including weightwatchers and over 45s, as well as iron-pumpers. Commented Chief Executive John Neill, 'A typical example of the Unipart spirit in action. An initial idea from one of our employees prompted a number of us to get together and develop a comprehensive plan for a fitness centre.'

OPEN TO ALL

An important motivating factor is that such centres should be open to all and Unipart stated firmly, 'We want everyone to feel equally welcome to Lean Machine whatever their position within the organisation.'

The centre is part of the global approach offered by the Group Occupational Health programme which covers help with diet, cutting down smoking and so on, and as well as helping people achieve a healthier life style would 'form a useful centre for the organisation of sporting and social events within the group.'

MOTIVATING A LOSS

Dan Lees was motivated to become fitter when a doctor described him as 'obese' which, as he was at the time a 19-stone weakling, was medically accurate.

He decided he would lose weight if he were to write a book for which he needed to try out a number of different energetic sports. Unfortunately most of the sportsmen, once they had finished introducing him to activities like abseiling, caving, wrestling and so on, proved so hospitable that he actually put on weight.

He then decided to write another book showing how a suitably motivated person could get fit in three months, by the end of which time he had lost 56lbs, become fit enough to put up a creditable showing in the *Sunday Times* Fun Run, and written a book called *The Champagne Fitness Book*.

More importantly he discovered a new zest for life – and for work. He was helped immensely by his local Fitness Centre where he discovered that some firms were either paying, or helping towards, the fees of their employees – a useful alternative to the capital expenditure involved in creating a corporate centre.

MOTIVATING BY SPORT

Involving the company in team games like football or hockey is another means of changing the culture, providing the whole of the workforce takes part in all the teams, rather than having, say, soccer for the shop floor and squash for the managers.

Even if you can't afford to provide private sports grounds you could encourage and back a netball team to play in the local park, or combine a useful motivation effort with some external PR by forming teams to play something unusual like petanque.

CASCADES AND EXPLOSIONS

All the above can help to erode the 'them' and 'us' culture but, like having everyone eat in the same canteen, the effects will be little more than cosmetic if the culture remains intact to the point where management feels the need to motivate 'them.' If this is the case, the most finely conceived cascades are in danger of becoming ineffectual driblets before they reach the final basin. Preaching to the already converted managers will help to re-motivate them and maintain their morale, but the effects could be totally dissipated by the time they reach the people whose culture most needs to be changed.

By contrast, grass roots motivation campaigns which involve everyone in the firm can produce enormous amounts of energy. It is when this energy is generated that the organisation should be in place to harness and direct it, by making sure that people's creativity, innovativeness, enthusiasm and hard work are seen to pay off for them and not just for the company – and to pay off for both on an ongoing basis.

Most of the great movements of history – both good and bad – have been inspired by a leader who motivated a small number of other leaders, not to cascade the message down through a hierarchy but to go among the foot soldiers, forming small groups and changing their culture until they became an unstoppable force.

TRAIN HARD – FIGHT EASY

As we have seen, the British Army, which is renowned for its high standards of professionalism, never stops training, and from the raw recruits to generals is dedicated to the need for continuous learning and improvement. The Japanese did not invent *kaizen* – only the word. Army physical training is hard and challenging – often to the limits of endurance – while education and theoretical training are available to take men and women as far as they wish to go, provided they have the capacity.

Until recently, industry mirrored the Army's pragmatic division of human material into rankers and officers, without much sign of anything like the Army's *repêchage* system, which attempts to ensure that potential senior officers don't slip through the net.

Now, the system of teamworking, quality circles and so on – in addition to being motivating in itself – is enabling management to spot future leaders, without the formal selection process which motivates only those chosen and leaves the rest demoralised.

MOTIVATING TRAINING

Training and education should begin with the induction programme which, as well as being good PR, ought to introduce the new recruit not merely to the company but to the company's culture. It can take the form of initial training, which includes lectures on the company package and the appointment of 'shadows' to provide help and encouragement in the early days, or a specific welcome package like the Worthing Health Authority's 'Welcome to Worthing'.

Faced with the need to combat inconsistent attendance and non-involvement by key departments in 'low profile', lack-lustre induction sessions, Worthing, which had a staff turnover rate as high as 45 per cent, has overhauled its induction process.

The present half-day programme introduces the Authority as an organisation with an annual budget of around £80 million, employing more than 4,000 people including doctors, nurses, midwives, allied professions and back up staff. It then brings in core values before moving on to sessions on Health and Safety and Fire Safety, an explanation of the pay slip and health promotion. Tutors have developed a more concise and punchy style; presentations, including a video, are better delivered, and there is a team quiz with a structured 'TV game' approach and a take-away information pack.

The induction is also seen as an opportunity for all branches and all levels of the organisation to get together – an exercise from which all parties can learn.

COMPANIES WITH UNIVERSITIES ATTACHED

At the other end of the training and education scale some companies, particularly hi-tech American firms, are now regarded as 'universities with companies attached'.

If everyone in the company is to be properly motivated the

journey between these two poles – from induction to higher education – should, for those capable of making it, be continuous.

The word 'career' is derived from a word meaning a carriage road, and managers should make sure all their employees know it is their intention to create career roads for all, with plenty of help available along the way and plenty of opportunities for changing direction or even for settling down.

STRUCTURING CONTINUOUS IMPROVEMENT

Motivating people to pursue continuous improvement is a good thing in itself but the effort has to be structured and managed.

Steve Tanner, for example, who as Quality Initiative Manager steered the staff of an Industrial Branch Unit to the achievement of BS5750, motivated them by making it an 'Event' and by showing them they could be winners. He also demonstrated this as their work was recomended under the Government National Training Award scheme.

Significantly, after the initial training was finished, staff continued to meet, to identify new problems and to solve them because, says Steve, the programme had been devised in such a way that 'it virtually stood as a new working practice in its own right.'

Now all staff receive instruction on the business world and customer care training which Steve describes as 'a development from Phase One which set the base.'

EDUCATING THE 'THEM' AND 'US'

Once the motivation pump has been primed, training and education are among the finest motivators of all as they provide ongoing satisfactions to suit every need from material gain to the opportunity for self-actualisation. They are the complete answer to the question of how to change the 'them' and 'us' culture, and to the legitimate question of both workers and management, i.e. What's in it for us?

WHAT'S IN IT FOR US?

Until quite recently – possibly as a survival from the days when it was fine to have money but not to earn it – British companies have been shy about profit. It was something which had to be mentioned in the balance sheet but, apart from that, one simply did not talk about it – especially in front of the workers,

This made some sort of sense in the days when workers had only to learn about profit being made to begin thinking in terms of 'trouble at t'mill.'

Now, however, the WHO? has changed to the point where workers are not only ready to face the economic facts of life regarding their own company, but may well have money in it which they wish to see earn a profit. This being the case, 'What's in it for us?' becomes not so much a declaration of war but a preliminary to negotiations.

NEGOTIATING A WIN-WIN SOLUTION

In a well motivated company everyone wins and nobody loses. This is known as a win–win situation and in sales, for instance, most managers now realise that winning by creating losers is a dangerously short sighted policy, which not only loses customers but can also ferment bitterness and a desire for revenge. A win–win is a genuine bargain which pleases both sides and creates not only a sale but a customer. Most managers now see suppliers as collaborators with whom it is essential to find a win–win solution.

Recently some managements, like many of those we have looked at, have begun to realise that their employees are among their most important suppliers and that if motivation is to be effective it must be seen to be leading towards a win–win situation. Some now go so far as to lay down in black and white, when introducing a new strategy, an audit of 'What's in it for you' and 'What's in it for us', and to make audio-visual presentations to their workforce as they would to any other supplier or customer.

A New Role for the Unions

In some companies the new relationship between management and employees has led to trade unions vanishing from the scene completely, which may not be altogether a good thing, as a well intentioned and honest management could be replaced by one favouring the CAS ratio of Genghis Khan virtually overnight.

Other trade unions have identified motivation as a Machiavellian management tool for getting more work out of employees for less money, and as such to be resisted at all costs. One major union has even made a video to help shop stewards combat insidious management motivation techniques like teamworking, quality circles and multi-skilling. In other cases the unions have adapted to a new role of watchdog, negotiators of win–win situations and enthusiastic fellow motivators whose aim is to ensure prosperity for their members by ensuring the prosperity of the company.

Company attitudes vary. In industries with a long history of bitterness and suspicion both sides find it difficult to change, while in those where relations have been merely strained, adapting to new ways is easier.

In the Unipart Group of Companies, for instance, there is now no union representation, while at Colt International the Managing Director Paul O'Hea now meets with union representatives twice a month and sees this development as an important breakthrough. In the Royal Mail the Chief Executive Bill Cockburn is convinced that co-existence is not only possible but highly desirable.

A Union View

Terry Gough, who is Chairman of the APEX Union at Colt International where he has worked for 23 years and been a member of the Union for 15 years, welcomes the end to permanent confrontation. 'If you go round all the companies and talk to all the union people you don't get so much talk these days of 'one out, all out' type confrontation.

'People are more willing to talk and everyone is seeking win–win solutions. We've come to the conclusion that after all these years of disruption strikes should be avoided wherever possible as damaging to both sides.'

At Colt, says Terry, where there is a tradition of management talking to workers, the relationship between the company and the union has always been good. 'Obviously we don't always get what we want – but they go out of their way to help us out, so we were quite willing for instance to go along with the motivation project and it has worked.

'Even here things have changed. This morning we had a meeting with our Director and the Personnel people about changing our PBR, Payment By Results, system. Some time ago everybody would have jumped about and said "No!" but today we all sat down and talked it over, and came up with some good ideas.'

Obviously, motivation is helping to change the culture of both 'them' and 'us' into the sort of 'we' which will be essential in the twenty-first century.

Summary

- The Ashridge Test. Employees are people.
- Changing the culture by helping the schools and by becoming an integral part of the local educational scene.
- Changing the culture by school visits, work experience for pre-school leavers. 'Open Days' and liaison with careers masters.
- Changing the culture by induction courses, family visits and 'shadows' and how induction courses should lead naturally to a career-long structure of education and training.
- How motivation is helping to change the culture of both management and employee.

Action

- Give yourself the Ashridge Test by first listing in order of importance all the things which motivate you. Then use the same list to place the factors in the order of importance you think they would have for your employees.

21. Motivating for the Twenty First Century

The 21st century is just around the corner and motivation is playing its part in ensuring that, by the time it arrives, people will have shed much of the cultural conditioning that has bedevilled management's relationship with the managed ever since the first hunter gatherers settled down to farming and manufacturing.

Employees have already become more responsive to management innovation and more inclined to use their intelligence and their enthusiasm on behalf of their employers rather than against them – provided they consider themselves adequately and suitably rewarded. Increasingly, they are demanding as part of the reward package that their work should be exciting, challenging, and enjoyable.

With this change in mind we can begin our look at the motivation of the future by asking once again with Herzberg 'How do you motivate employees?'

How do you Motivate the New Type of Employee?

As employee attitudes change in the direction of a Theory Y culture of people keen to earn the rewards that are their due, how can you channel this new enthusiasm? How should you motivate people who think of work as something to be enjoyed? The answer lies in a return to the natural Pleasure Principle by which the first leaders motivated teams of hunters at the time of the hunter gatherers.

- **Be Enthusiastic and Responsive to Motivation Yourself**

Only an enthusiastic leader is capable of inspiring and motivating others. An enthusiastic leader will also be prepared to be a visible leader, to mix with the foot soldiers and have a thorough knowledge of their jobs, while recognising that it is they who have the expertise. Like the leader of a hunting band the genuine leader is motivated by the joys, the risks and the necessities of the task, he is wise in the lore of his particular business but does not pretend to know better than every single member of his group. It is his function as leader to weld them into a harmonious and efficient team.

- **Choose People who will be Responsive to your Motivation**

The leader of a hunting party would perhaps have used a mixture of threats and promises to motivate hunters he knew to be merely idle. He would not have wasted time on people who hated the effort and the risks of the hunt. He would have picked the best and most enthusiastic hunters for his team, and would have left the others to a less active task that suited them better.

Take the opportunity when you are hiring, to hire the best, even at the lowest level in your organisation. Everything else being equal, choose the shopfloor employee who welcomes the idea of up-skilling and the junior executive who asks about training courses as well as salary and benefits. Remember, if you are recruiting now, you could well be seeking to motivate the person concerned in the third Millenium. If you have employees who are happy in undemanding, routine jobs, show them that there is a way out, but allow them to make the final choice.

- **Treat Each Situation on its Merits**

Motivating a group to hunt tree squirrels would have presented different problems to those of motivating a lion hunt.

Use the five W Questions to establish the Who?, What?, Why?' When? and Where? before tackling the How?.

Remember that while the people you are seeking to motivate will be very much like you, their background may be unlike yours and could in fact be completely different. This will become increasingly the case as we move toward the twenty-first century and the globe becomes even more of a village because, as people like Geert Rofstede have pointed out, culture-determined value systems have to be taken into account when transferring management ideas from one country to another – even within Europe – and this applies particularly to motivation.

• Set Specific and Realisable Targets

Hunting parties were not open-ended, either in their aims or the time taken to accomplish them. Hunters knew that they were aiming to bring down as much food as they could carry over a limited distance. Both success and failure were easily identified.

Challenges are motivating but they should be specific and realisable within a set time limit. Open-ended calls for 'More' and 'Better' have very little motivating power compared with three month, six month or one year achievable targets and well thought out and mutually agreed plans to reach them.

Employees who, for example, would find it unsettling and unfair to be asked to achieve 'more production and better quality', will respond more positively to the challenge posed by the problem of producing ten per cent more goods with five per cent fewer rejects or remakes within the year.

• Remember that 'Getting There' Motivates

For the hunters – and the gatherers – success meant immediate celebration, as there were few means of deferring pleasures. Success is a matter of pride. Achieving targets provides its own satisfaction.

Achieving quality, especially, implies a return to craftmanship and the satisfactions which motivated people to create artefacts that were also works of art.

Set intermediate targets on the way to the major achievement so that you and your people can celebrate every success on the way and build up a head of steam for the challenges ahead.

● Create a Motivating Environment

The first hunter gatherers already had a motivating environment. Theirs has been described by anthropologists as 'the first affluent society', in which nature provided plenty for all with no pollution, very little stress and only the friendliest of competition. Now managers control the working environment, so don't ask people to work in conditions or with equipment that you would spurn if they were offered to you. You are motivating people to give of their best, so give them a place they can look forward to working in. If you get a kick out of showing friends, customers and competitors the conditions under which your people work you are probably on the right lines.

Don't forget the human element. If possible, give people a chance to move out of a human environment which they find de-motivating. An ongoing clash of temperaments can harm your organisation and ruin your motivation efforts.

● Provide Fair and Appropriate Rewards

For the hunters the product of their work was a reward in itself and its prime motivation.

Today's employees, no matter how responsive to factors higher up in the needs hierarchy, still have to 'bring back the bacon' and before tackling any form of motivation it is essential to get the money right. This is especially the case in respect of the lower echelons who should be making at least the average for your particular industry, before financial incentives as such are considered.

Even where this is the case the practice of some Japanese

companies who, in order to maintain discipline and promote teamworking, make additions to the norm contingent on individual assessment as well as the achievement of production targets, is about as much 'stick' motivation as 21st century employees are likely to put up with.

• Provide Recognition

For hunters half the pleasure of the chase lies in the applause and admiration of other hunters. In the same way peer approval and the recognition of our efforts by hierarchic superiors are among the most powerful motivators.

It is good manners to say 'thank you' if someone performs a small service; how much more so if the person concerned contributes hard work, skill and ideas to the improvement of your company.

By definition, an 'employee' is involved in the organisation he or she works for and, in the same way, an employer is one who 'implicates', or involves. Making that involvement meaningful by recognising it, utilising it and building on it, will enable you to release a virtually limitless source of energy and an immense 'NET motivation in the desired direction.'

WHAT'S IN IT FOR ME?

So why should I make work more enjoyable for my people? They are not primitive huntsmen who are motivated by pleasure, but employees who sell their time and labour in exchange for wages. I pay them good money, so why should I bother to do anything else, now or in the future?

The indications are that an increasingly large proportion of the workforce is becoming responsive to non-financial motivation. If the companies and organisations we have investigated and consulted are anything to go by, sound motivation practices can lead to: better morale, improved industrial relations, greater efficiency, higher productivity, better quality and less waste, leading to greater profits. In some cases managers reported that a high percentage of their increase in profits – 80 per cent in one case – was directly attributable to their motivation efforts.

Managers who deliver these sort of results are motivating themselves into a bright future in the 21st century.

So What's the Downside? – Where's the Catch?

A fair question, especially as some of the successes obtained by the best motivation practice seem almost too good to be true.

In fact, they are the logical result of getting everyone in the team to pull in the same direction rather than every which way.

However there is a downside, in that, unless you 'pay as you go', you can continue motivating for just so long before your employees begin to ask 'And what about the workers?'

Negative Synergy and the Motivating-isms

Much worse is the fact that, because of what appears to be some form of negative synergy, the collapse of an unfulfilled motivating effort produces an effect far greater than one which is merely 'equal and opposite.'

The Soviet system which ruled over a Communist empire for nearly three-quarters of a century was marvellously motivated. They had what appeared to be a noble cause, an inspiring idea and total control of their citizens from the cradle to the grave. Motivation was the keynote of their education system from infant school onward, while a multi-million strong youth organisation, the Komsomol, concentrated all its energies on producing dedicated, well trained and highly motivated leaders who would inspire and motivate the whole population. At first the highly motivated population was asked to work hard and make sacrifices for the idea and ideals of Communism. When this palled a little – only to be rekindled by the Great Patriotic War, the Russian term for World War Two, – the Communist motivators turned to the concept of the target and

Russians were told that they were working on a Five Year Plan, at the end of which things would be a great deal better.

THE MOTIVATORS WHO PROMISED TOO MUCH

Sadly, at the end of the five years, no matter how much the government attempted to tell people that things had improved, they patently had not.

Another bigger and better Five Year Plan was announced with similar results – and another – and another, until people at last began to notice that, although things had scarcely improved for them, they had certainly improved for those who were doing all the motivating – the nomenklatura or Party bosses who had cars, dachas and goods from the *beriozka* shops otherwise reserved for hard currency purchasers. Suddenly the Russians became not simply un-motivated but motivated in what, from their leaders' point of view, was an undesired direction, which led them to dismantle an empire and a regime.

It is no use motivating people unless at the same time you provide them with the means to accomplish the set tasks, the opportunity to fulfil them and firm evidence that your motivating effort is based on achievable rewards.

THE HIGHLY MOTIVATED NAZIS

Further proof that motivation is not the sole prerogative of the good was provided by Hitler, one of the great motivators of all time who motivated a bunch of outcasts to take over a country and went on to motivate the country to a point where it very nearly took over the world.

Hitler's appreciation of what motivating buttons to press bordered on the uncanny. In fact, he got almost everything right. He was responsive to all the motivations he used on others, he selected people he could motivate, and was adroit in motivating different sections of the German nation in different ways. He even managed to motivate a surprising number of seemingly ordinary individuals to commit unspeakable atrocities.

Ostensibly, his first targets were realistic and challenging and resulted in motivating progress in the shape of territorial expansion, national pride, motorways and material prosperity. Rewards and recognition were a Nazi speciality, as were punishments – usually fatal – for those whose motivation appeared unsound.

For a long time, as sacrifices and effort brought victory after victory, it appeared that Hitler would deliver on his promises. Unfortunately for him he had over-motivated without fully providing the opportunities and the means, so that when he failed to deliver on his biggest and most solemn promise to win final victory, the German nation didn't just become less motivated but lapsed into complete demoralisation.

Motivating Promises Must be Kept

The implication for managers is that motivation by ideas can achieve miracles but that in the end the motivators have to deliver. If you promise your employees a better future, more money, more involvement, or a better company car, sooner or later – and preferably sooner – you are going to have to deliver or face consequences much graver than a mere reversal of your motivating efforts.

With that in mind, you can go on to achieve miracles of motivation if your ideas appeal to the people you wish to motivate, especially if your idea is one which is based, however tenuously, on a 'noble cause'.

'Sell the Sizzle – Not the Sausage'

Advertisers, who are expert and professional motivators, sell the idea of the product and not the product itself, but they realise that if, in the end, the products they sell fail to satisfy the customers they will only buy once. In much the same way, enthusiastic motivators can 'sell' their employees on an idea, but it must be the right idea, and in the end it has to work – for all concerned.

ANOTHER FAILED-ISM

Another idea which has failed, though less spectacularly than fascism or communism, is the sort of rapacious, uncaring capitalism which gave business a bad name from the start of the Industrial Revolution, and which has reared its head on occasions ever since – as laissez-faire capitalism or the 'gimme' culture.

This culture, which favours a horse and buggy style of motivation based on primitive carrot and stick methods, with a CAS ratio heavily loaded towards 'stick', runs counter to the great emotional tides of the late twentieth century. It is the capitalism of the robber barons and the Mafia, successful only as long as it can keep people in a state of fear.

THE CHANGING CULTURE OF MANAGEMENT

We have talked a great deal about the changing culture of employees and how, often with the encouragement of motivating leadership, they are gradually abandoning attitudes based on centuries of conditioning in favour of a more responsive and co-operative posture. Certainly they are no longer the cowed, resentful creatures of the Satanic Mills.

What is equally important is that the culture of the managers has changed even faster, so that most ironmasters or mill owners of a hundred years ago would be totally out of place in a modern enterprise. Now, even the leader who knows only how to inspire his troops is rapidly becoming an anachronism and the new manager is not only learning to motivate but to structure motivation.

STRUCTURED MOTIVATION MANAGEMENT

There was a time when changing the CAS ratio of an organisation to suit the changing culture of employees was sufficient to give companies an edge.

Then, as the 'stick' factors were used less and less, the 'carrot' factors became more sophisticated to the point where employees were increasingly involved in the business of their organisation. This led to more and more team working, quality circles and the like, the effects of which on job satisfaction, productivity and morale were frequently little short of miraculous. So much so, that the teams themselves seemed to be magic circles bringing almost instant success to all who used them.

In the general atmosphere of euphoria hardly anyone seemed to notice that the teams and circles were motivated by: (1) the Hawthorne effect – which ensures that merely being noticed motivates employees to perform better (2) by aims like 'Total Quality', which as a noble cause is also highly motivating, and (3) by merely being teams.

Nor did everyone notice that those organisations which fully enjoyed the benefits of a motivation miracle were those that had a structure in place which enabled them to manage, direct and sustain the energy that was being generated.

Structured motivation allows employees to own the problems they can handle and to develop the ability to handle more, while keeping the manager firmly in control. This control will become even more important for many managers of the future who will need all their organisational and people skills to create and direct multi-disciplined teams – brought together to assess, plan and complete specific tasks – which many motivation experts see as the logical development of 'teamworking'.

THE NEW MANAGER

Today's manager has not only changed his attitudes towards his employees. He has changed his attitudes to life, bringing his own motivation and the ways in which he motivates his employees into line with late twentieth century trends.

Many of the top motivators are concerned for example with Green issues, with the impact of their business on the community, with good works and with charity. Some firms are giving a fixed percentage of their profits to charitable causes at home and abroad, some are backing employees' efforts to take aid to the Third World, while others help in small but important ways by allowing their employees to take part in civic activities, like becoming blood donors, in the firm's time.

In addition to this change in attitude, the modern manager is better educated, better read, better informed and better trained than his predecessors. His motivation will usually be different from that of his predecessors, which is just as well, as managers will be a great deal more powerful, both as individuals and as a body, than any managers before them.

THE POWER OF THE NEW MANAGERS

Now machines are placing undreamed of power in the hands of the new managers, powers which can be multiplied by motivating the employees who man the machines and by the synergetic effects of the communications revolution.

Already managers – using electronic mail, phones and fax – can cross borders and frontiers with greater speed and more effect than the pilots of jet fighters.

Already there are world-wide companies with budgets larger than some nation states, often with better trained and more charismatic leaders. The implications are clear: the manager of the 21st century will have a bigger say in how the world is organised and run than ever before, and this is why his motivation, and that which he passes on to his troops, must be sound.

MOTIVATING BY DREAMS

Dreams are the most powerful motivators of all and men or women with a great enough dream, if they can find people to share it, can motivate the world, because dreams make the world an exciting place in which to live and work.

'I have a dream,' said Martin Luther King, crystalising for all time the idea of the motivating vision and its power to stir human emotions. We all need a vision, something bigger than ourselves, to carry us beyond self-actualisation, towards what Samuel Johnson called 'the desire of good'.

Fortunately, whether we are managers or managed, we don't need to be saints in order to be motivated by 'the desire of good'. It is quite sufficient to be a normal human being with those human needs for love, affection, approval and accomplishment that make a person strive to become an all-round winner, not just in the workplace but in the whole of life.

The Challenges of Peace

The great challenge which faces all leaders and managers, and which is becoming more acute as more and more people begin to demand more stimulating and pleasurable lives, is to make peace and its profitable occupations as exciting as war.

This is being achieved in part by empowering individuals to control their own working lives and to share to some extent both in the achievement and the risk taking, for a long time the prerogative of management.

Most people will work hard for reasonable pay, but they will play even harder just for the hell of it, often competing for the sake of the challenge, the applause or the enjoyment of risking the smallest of stakes and they will play even harder if their game is somehow linked to a cause.

Fittingly, the answer to the whole question of how to motivate now and in the future comes not from a guru but from a group of Royal Mail front line teamworkers whose exhibition stand slogan expressed perfectly the idea of a return to the Pleasure Principle:

Somehow, we must find ways for ourselves and others 'to have fun – and make the world a better place.'

Further Reading

Adair J. (1988) *The Action Centred Leader*, London: The Industrial Society; *Great Leaders* (1989) Talbot Adair Press; *Understanding Motivation* (1990) Talbot Adair Press

Barham K. and Oates D. (1991) *The International Manager*, London: Century

Calero H. and Oskam B. (1988) *Negotiate for What You Want*, London: Thorsons

Dalton G. (1974) *Economic Systems and Society*, London: Penguin

Dixon N. F. (1988) *On the Psychology of Military Incompetence*, London: Futura

Herzberg F. (1966) *Work and the Nature of Man*, World Publishing; 'One More time: How Do You Motivate Employees?', article in Harvard Business Review, 1968

Kanter R. M. (1989) *When Giants Learn to Dance*, New York: Simon and Schuster

Kennedy C. (1991) *Guide to the Management Gurus*, London: Century Business

Leakey R. E. (1981) *The Making of Mankind*, London: Michael Joseph

Lloyd H. and Lloyd P. (1981) *Teach Yourself Public Relations*, London: Hodder and Stoughton

Macdonald L. (1983) *Somme*, London: Michael Joseph

McGregor D. (1960) *The Human Side of Enterprise*, Maidenhead: McGraw-Hill

Maslow A. H. (1970) *Motivation and Personality*, New York: Harper and Row

Mayo E. (1933) *The Human Problems of an Industrial Civilisation*, London: Macmillan

O'Connor J. and Seymour J. (1990) *Introducing Neuro-Linguistic Programming*, Crucible

Peters T. and Waterman R. (1982) *In Search of Excellence*, New York: Harper and Row

Rodgers F. G. and Shook R. L. (1986) *The IBM Way*, New York: Harper and Row

Ross P. with Samson D. (1989) *Ask For the Moon and Get It*, London: Thorsons

Russell, Bertrand (1984) *A History of Western Philosophy*, London: Unwin

Schonberger R. J. (1990) *Building a Chain of Customers*, London: Century Business

Townsend R. (1984) *Further Up the Organisation*, London: Michael Joseph

Vroom, V. H. (1964) *Work and Motivation*, Chichester: John Wiley

Wilmshurst J. (1985) *The Fundamentals of Advertising*, London: Butterworth Heinemann

Index